No Easy Answers

Barbara Baisley

No Easy Answers

An Exploration of Suffering

EPWORTH PRESS

0 7162 0539 4

First published 2000
by Epworth Press
20 Ivatt Way
Peterborough, PE3 7PG

Typeset by Regent Typesetting, London
Printed and bound in Great Britain by
Biddles Ltd, Guildford and King's Lynn

To Reg

Contents

Foreword

by the Right Reverend Colin Bennetts

Bishop of Coventry

Barbara asks a very pertinent question in the introduction to her book: 'What are we to do with suffering when it comes?' Perhaps another way of asking the question is, 'What are we to be when suffering comes?' This compelling story, charting as it does the agony and anguish of pain and suffering, reveals a God who enters into the experience, right alongside us. But he doesn't just stand there. If we allow him to, he will use such experiences of suffering so that ultimately we can say, as Barbara did, that in whatever guise it comes, suffering is a peculiar, horrible and yet precious gift, transforming us into the people God wants us to be.

This is a compelling and yet humbling book. Read it if you dare, and allow this whole new approach to suffering transform your life.

Introduction

I have cancer – but that is not what this book is about, or
rather, cancer is not the point. Perhaps if the disease had not
recurred the memories would have faded. They would have
become *a bad patch,* to look back on complacently as a close
shave. But as an on-going situation, cancer constantly and
persistently challenges my faith and threatens my security. I
hope that what I have to say will relate to a variety of different
circumstances. I offer my story, not because it is particularly
tragic or heroic, but because the experience has shaken me as
nothing else in my life. I have been forced to ask – what we are
to *do* with suffering when it comes? How are we to bear the
pain and uncertainty? Is it possible to use suffering in some
way, or let ourselves be used in it?

I know that my thoughts can offer no ultimate answer.
Perhaps they are more of a jumping off point, an encouragement in the search we all engage in when life knocks us and
leaves us flailing. For you it is a different battle: perhaps
another disease or disability, the death of a loved one, family
breakdown or an unwelcome move. Each of us encounters
times when we wrestle with the age-old chestnuts: Why *me*?
How can there be a good God when such horrors exist and
persist? For me the questions have been caused by breast
cancer which has spread to my skeleton, though not yet any
further. I am well aware that this has not been the worst that
can happen. I am not dead, not paralysed, not alone, not even
currently in great pain. But sometimes I try to imagine things
as they were, as they might have been; and then I realize how
totally cancer has dominated my life over these fourteen years.

'If only . . .', I grieve. 'How wonderful to be released from the menace, to be able to forget the disease completely and be free.' And yet, there is another part of me that knows that the experience has shaped me and made me what I am. Cancer has given me its own peculiar, horrible, yet precious gift. I cannot go back and in a sense, on good days, I would not wish to.

I

Cancer – The Shock

Initially I only wanted to hide. I had returned for the results of tests, having discovered a lump in my breast two weeks before, and lay stripped on a couch, embarrassed and exposed, as the Consultant emerged from his inner sanctum. I knew by his face that he had bad news and that he didn't want to have to tell me. The lump was malignant and had to be removed. 'We'll do a segmented mastectomy,' he explained, 'less devastating than removing the whole breast.' I remember vividly my sense of total unreality. I smiled brightly, stupidly, as I had learnt to do from an early age: hide your distress, don't let them see the hurt; it's more manageable that way.

Somebody named as The Breast Sister stayed with me. Probably she was a pleasant and sympathetic person. I found her obnoxious. She was cheery and, unforgivably, seemed to have two whole breasts. I wanted to tell her to take her patronizing smile and jump in a river. No doubt I was placatory and polite; all I wanted was for her to go away. She chatted about a prosthesis, and I had not the slightest idea what she meant. She said probably a hankie down my bra would do just as well, and I wanted to shout obscenities and scratch her face. I simpered and looked brave and cheerful, waiting, willing her to go. I kept thinking – this can't be happening, we don't have cancer in our family! Obviously my mother's emphasis on good thoughts and regular bowel action as mainstays of life had influenced me more than I thought! The Breast Sister continued: 'What about my lifestyle, was I a tense person?' Silly cow, I run on adrenalin, I thought. 'Perhaps I should think about re-prioritizing' – or maybe about dying, I added privately. 'Yes,' I said, 'Well, I'll think about it, thank you very much.' You harpy, you witch, you bitch! I screamed inside my head. I felt an overwhelming need to get up and be dressed and out of the room; a desire to run, to turn back the day, not to know, not have to face it.

All of this was written down in a journal some three years later. I was trying at that time to find some perspective on the experience, in an attempt to put it behind me. Looking back now, I wonder how much of the anger I recorded belonged to this *making sense*, long after I had received the first news. I can still clearly remember the sense of wanting to run, but I think I was too stunned for a great deal of emotion. Writing about the event later I felt the fury and outrage, but at the time only shock, frozen terror and the need to flee. I was thirty-nine and had been in my ideal job for a year. I felt that I was just at the beginning and now had suddenly come to an end.

Over the next weeks and months I veered from shock to terror, anger to despair. The treatment, removing a segment of my breast followed by radiotherapy, was straightforward and I was told that the prognosis was good. I did not ask many questions, mainly because I did not know what to ask. I was an outsider in an unknown world with its own language, and my basic confidence in life was shattered. I had only one question – or rather ten thousand, all meaning the same thing: 'Am I going to die?' In my head the questions never stopped, but chased each other in an endless riddle: 'Will it come back? Why don't you know? Who does? What do you *really* think? When will someone know? How will I know if something is wrong? How will *you* know? Why can't you tell for sure? How could this happen to me? What will happen if I die? Why me? Why Barbara?' The nearest I got to expressing any of this was at an early check-up with the oncologist. 'Would you tell me if you found something else?' I asked timidly. I was convinced that any recurrence of cancer meant immediate removal to a Hospice to await death in an atmosphere of hushed evasion of the truth. He laughed and said that naturally I would be told, as I would have to receive treatment. He was kind and meant to reassure me, but I felt a fool. He could not know about the fantasies of deathbed scenes that lay behind my question. It did not occur to me to ask him to sit down and talk to me about the probable course of the disease: how cancer works; why it acts the way it does; what sort of secondaries might occur; how long I might survive if the disease did return; how I could help myself? And probably any answers and explanations would have been incomprehensible; the little I was told had been difficult to take in. I was in pieces and ashamed of my inability to deal with my feelings and my fears.

My diagnosis came a fortnight before Christmas. In the first moments of panic, I had asked to wait until the New Year before going in for the operation. It seemed inconceivable that my life should be interrupted in this way and instinctively I wanted to continue with the normal pattern of Christmas, arguing that I was protecting our teenage sons. No doubt I was trying to protect myself, too! The three-week interval before the operation was not easy. I had read about the need to demystify cancer and wanted to be open with everyone, but I did not understand that I needed time to face my own re-actions. I had not yet absorbed the news and simply could not believe what was happening. So the Christmas preparations and celebrations continued, my father and our sons were told, the Belgian exchange student arrived as arranged, and the usual visitors packed into the rectory for Christmas. I took a full part in the services, smiling desperately. I wanted to believe that I was being sensible and positive and that I could cope. It seemed very important that everyone else believe that too, but I did not ask myself why.

People tried to be kind. There were those who gave hearty encouragement: 'My mother, friend, cousin had the same thing and died of a heart attack at eighty-three, or had no trouble for sixteen years.' Others took a down-to-earth, no nonsense approach: 'One in eight women has breast cancer, it is commonplace and nothing to worry about.' All these remarks made me feel I was making a fuss about nothing. Not that I *was* making a fuss. Outwardly I was cheerful and stoic, inwardly I was in chaos. Some friends tried to boost me in terms of my faith. 'Of course, you'll come flying through – God will look after his own!' But this too seemed to make light of my fear and reproach my lack of certainty. I felt misunderstood and my face ached with smiling. On the other hand, the obvious horror of one acquaintance terrified me as she graphically related the story of her friend whose breast cancer had killed her within a year. In a few sentences she destroyed the fragile peace of mind I had managed to muster for that day. It was hard for anyone to get it right!

Cancer terrifies and mesmerizes us as one of the last unbeaten fatal diseases. Whenever I have to say, 'I have cancer,' I wait for the sudden stillness, as if I have said something obscene or started to take my clothes off. It is not unlike the reaction when I am asked what I do, at the hairdressers or a party. 'I am a priest, actually,' I say, with a big *normal*, reassuring smile, but usually meet a similar embarrassed hush. The fact that cancer inspires such horror has spawned a thousand theories about its cause and treatment; diets and meditation, homeopathy, massage, visualization, hypnosis, vitamins and positive thinking, to name a few. Everyone has an opinion and favourite treatment and I have found the weight of advice offered by kind, well-meaning people almost as heavy a burden as the disease itself. I understand that the endless list of causes and therapies is the result of people's longing to help, to do something. All of which makes it impossible to respond as I have sometimes needed to, with well-chosen expletives!

Initially, I found it hard to rest or to give myself any permission to feel bad, physically or emotionally. I thought this was taking a positive attitude. I avoided programmes about cancer; advice and helpful literature were ignored; I did not want to know. I was determined not to change my frenetic lifestyle and desperate to remain in control. To be unable to cope seemed the worst failure. 'I'm fine,' I insisted, not in a deliberate attempt to deceive but because I did not know what else to say. I was disorientated and often could not tell how I felt. 'I'm fine' seemed the safest response.

There was enormous emphasis in my upbringing on being cheerful and positive. As children we were regularly exhorted to be grateful for our good home, school and health, not to mention the cabbage or liver in front of us, whose health-giving properties had prompted the discussion. As the youngest of three, by several years, I was very conscious of having to keep up with the others and of being expected to ignore minor knocks and grazes. Any whining on my part was mocked and recitations of 'It's not fair' were firmly sat upon. This early training was reinforced by my role in the church and no doubt played a part of my leaning towards a caring profession. I wanted to be and appear capable and strong and early in life had learnt to hide hurts behind a breezy exterior. My ingrained attitude was no advantage now. It merely stopped me recognizing how devastated I felt.

Despite coming from a generation when careers for girls were listed as teaching, secretarial work or nursing, I had never felt any inclination to rustle about in a starched uniform, although I was definitely sold on the idea of saving people. My imagination fed on the historical novels I devoured and I longed for adventure and deeds of heroism. Hours and days in my childhood were spent picturing myself beating back flames, or galloping across enemy countryside with secret messages. Soothing fevered brows, however, had never attracted me; on the contrary, I found illness repellent. The fantasy world, where I figured as the conquering hero, no doubt fed my rather dubious inclination to do good to people: but my interest was in people as people. I wanted to know about their hopes, their dreads and their attempts to make sense of life, never about their bodies. It was not that I had not considered the question of suffering, but I thought of it as something abstract.

In the winter of 1986, when I was first diagnosed with breast cancer, I was a deaconess (women priests in the Church of England came eight years later), and the chaplain at the

University of Warwick. I had written essays on the subject of suffering at theological college and, having looked at some of my own inner turmoils and taken a variety of counselling courses, I privately considered myself rather an expert. A large part of my work was listening to students endlessly recounting their own troubles, as well as dissecting the problems of a painful world. Emotional discomfort did not frighten me, or so I thought, but physical ills were another matter.

Until this point I had simply considered my health as given. My body was not athletic or particularly disciplined, but it had never caused me any trouble. Indeed I had little interest in it beyond expecting it to perform efficiently and to look reasonably acceptable to the rest of the world. My knowledge of cancer was limited to understanding that I should check my breasts now and then for lumps. Beyond that I had a general impression that one was either cured by surgery, or headed swiftly for an early grave. I certainly had no conception of cancer as an ongoing condition. Now, fourteen years after cancer was first diagnosed, I have had to revise my prejudices against illness, hospitals, the nursing profession and the weaknesses of the human flesh.

Looking back, I can see that my first reactions of shock and denial were entirely normal and healthy, although at the time they seemed to be a signal of breakdown. In a moment of insight some four years later, and just after the cancer first reappeared in the lymph system, I wrote: *I have written pages of questions, doubts and fears in the last few days. It seems that just as I was leaving cancer behind, everything has fallen apart again.* George (my husband) *says that all this is natural, that it is inevitable that I rework the ground. I have suddenly realized how like bereavement this is – the constant talking about the dead one, over and over – and gradually, only gradually, letting it rest. So it has been with cancer. I am not wrong, a failure, without faith, to keep on at it. I think I should have an answer, but I am still in it, still working, still newly bereaved – all over again. And so I go round and round, telling the story, trying to make sense and to take it in.*

A sudden disaster will always meet us as a kind of bereavement. Whether we encounter news of cancer, divorce, tragedy or death, we are faced with a loss of our certainties, our opportunities, or the future we had imagined. Bewildered and in pain, we grieve for our past securities and lost routine. We mourn the life that was ours yesterday. Those who have studied the process of bereavement speak of four distinct stages of grief, although it is true that each person is different and will not necessarily follow any orderly progression through the process. Some will spend long periods in a particular stage, while for others stages may merge together. But some of the different emotions will generally be present and have certainly been part of my own reactions to cancer.

Faced with a deep trauma, we are initially in shock, disorientated and frequently our feelings are numb. Later comes anger, the need to blame someone or something for what has happened, often ourselves. We wrestle with irrational guilt and look for targets for our distress. Angry when we find an identifiable cause, we are equally angry if we cannot. Later still we become acutely aware of the pain of loss and may fall into depression, endlessly searching for the one who is gone or struggling with a sense of pointlessness. It is not until some parts of these different stages are faced and felt that we can move to an acceptance of the situation and come to some sort of peace.

This book is an attempt to trace my own wandering course through these stages of grief, although for much of the time I have been unaware of making a journey, and I have not yet reached the end. Cancer is something of a cat and mouse experience; the disease is unpredictable and may appear to go away completely but then recur, sometimes after years. This complicates life for those of us struggling to make sense of our situation because we never know where we are. Being *within* the experience, I have not found it easy to recognize that I have been travelling forwards, rather than round in circles. It is only now, after a number of years, that I can at last distinguish some landmarks and see that the shock, grief and anger, the blaming myself and others, the questions and searching for meaning have been part of a journey. Rather than tell my story in chronological order, the following pages explore various themes that relate to my own erratic progress. I hope that in this way my experience might connect more easily with others who are also looking for ways to move forward. However often we find ourselves apparently back at the beginning, repeating the questions, we are journeying. We may sometimes need a gentle nudge, but usually, if we are honest with ourselves and sufficiently patient, we will glimpse some light ahead, however feeble and flickering, and move on.

My journey is also complicated by the need to include God. Because I am a Christian, my questions and much of my anger have consciously been about God and directed towards God. I have tried to discover connections with others, whether in the Bible or in Christian tradition, who have wrestled with the fact of God. For the problem is universal: how to believe in a good God when the questions are hard and the nights long.

When I first learned that I had cancer, although I understood the theory about the grief process, I had no idea that I had suffered a bereavement. I only knew that I felt hurt and bewildered. Over the years of living with cancer I have realized that any query about my condition always comes as a shock and will take me back to where I started. I may think I have come to terms with my situation, I am used to speaking about cancer and feel acclimatized, but the experience is always different, raw and horrible in its own particular way. A new process of medical investigation always brings an initial sense of disorientation, shock, a new bereavement. It is rather like an endless game of Snakes and Ladders. I am doing well and have the questions neatly packaged with the answers, when the dice suddenly lands me on the wrong square and I find myself back down the snake again. Except that it is not quite the beginning: imperceptibly we edge forwards.

'No one ever told me that grief felt so like fear,' begins C. S. Lewis, writing of the death of his wife. He goes on to describe his feelings of shock, despite the fact that her death was long expected:

> I find it hard to take in what anyone says. Or perhaps, hard to want to take it in. It is so uninteresting. Yet I want others to be about me. I dread the moments when the house is empty. If only they would talk to one another and not to me.[1]

I wanted to turn his first words round: 'No one ever told me that fear felt so like grief!' Fear was what dominated me, the over-riding emotion that seemed to swallow everything, my breath, my confidence and sense of control. And, worse, I was ashamed of my fears. I was a Christian minister and felt I had no business being afraid of illness or the possibility of death. After all we declare week by week that Christ is risen and death defeated. Of all people, surely the threat of death should be of little consequence to me! The painful realization was that neither reasoning nor faith were much help. I was afraid and I felt that God had betrayed me. 'Wasn't I doing my best?' I remember protesting, as if I were being punished for some unknown sin. Had I been listening to someone else express such thoughts, I would have reassured them and said their confusion and fear were normal and even healthy. But it was different being in the grip of these disorientating emotions and frightening not feeling in control.

Early on I did not begin to wrestle with the big questions of 'Why' and 'Whose fault is it?' My first problem was that I had assumed that when we are in trouble, real trouble, God is there for us. Not that I had been constantly aware of God's presence in the past. On the contrary, discovering a sense of God's loving care for me had been slow and was still patchy. But I had come to realize that this was largely due to my insecurities and distorted childhood idea of an angry, condemning God. Despite these difficulties, I had always assumed that God would show up if I were in *real* need. That whatever my doubts and failings, the rescue would come in the final reel. It certainly did not feel like that. C. S. Lewis experienced the same sense of abandonment in his bereavement:

> Meanwhile, where is God? This is one of the most disquieting symptoms. When you are happy, so happy that you have no sense of needing Him, so happy that you are tempted to feel his claims on you as an interruption, if you remember yourself and turn to Him with gratitude and praise, you will be – or so it feels – welcomed with open arms. But go to Him when your need is desperate, when all other help is vain, and what do you find? A door slammed in your face, and a sound of bolting and double bolting on the inside.[2]

That was the real trouble. My world was shattered and the hymns and comforting Bible verses were no use. They only seemed to accuse me, suggesting that I should know God's love as never before, rest on his promises and stand firm in his peace. But I was afraid. The certainties that I had relied on had disappeared. I had always assumed that my children would be born normal and that life would continue, fulfilling and healthy well into my seventies – by which time I would be wise enough to cope with my mortality. In short I had thought that nothing really frightening would ever happen to me and that I was safe. Now I felt sabotaged, isolated and unable to admit it.

After surgery came the further shock of facing disfigurement. I had been warned that I must not mind my appearance and told, quite rightly, that in time the breast would look almost normal. But nothing could have prepared me for the shock: *This little apology for a breast, is me? It's a joke, an obscenity, like a pyramid stitched with twine – bruised black and yellow, the skin puckered and punctured – it bears no resemblance to the fullness and weight of a breast! I am not the same, not whole any more.* The following day, I added: *I feel low and exhausted, I spent the night going through various scenarios of being told the cancer is terminal. I don't know how to cope with this endless uncertainty.* I had expected the fear to end after the operation and that, once the episode was over, life would resume as if cancer had never been diagnosed. Gradually it dawned on me that this was not possible. *I bawled my eyes out in George's visit,* I wrote. *'I'm a mess, not a real woman. God has let me down. Is he mocking me, playing some game?'* *George tried hard to convince me that there is no cancer in my body, that it would have been found, that I am safe. Then he said a prayer for me about Jesus being disfigured too and for some reason that helped.*

But not for long. I could be comforted, but no amount of encouragement lasted. I waited for a return to normality, assuming that as the scar healed and I recovered from radiotherapy, the shock would fade and life continue as it had done. Although outwardly this is what happened, I discovered that inwardly this was not possible, nothing was the same. I wrote pages of lament in my journal: *We watched* The Graduate *on TV last night, and got to the bit where Dustin Hoffman fondles Anne Bancroft's breast. I burst into tears – 'I could never seduce anyone, now!' George was fed up, he just wanted to watch the film. I suppose he's heard it all! Later he was sweet and told me I am beautiful, to go on being me. I am so tired. I just want to be left to curl up and die. I don't want to see anyone or do anything. I can't face today.* I wallowed in self-pity, with only occasional flickers of faith, except that if the journal is addressed to anyone, it is to God.

C. S. Lewis talks about the intensity of our need being the barrier with God:

I have gradually been coming to see that the door is no longer shut and bolted. Was it my own frantic need that slammed it in my face? The time when there is nothing at all in your soul except a cry for help may be just the time when God can't give it: you are like the drowning man who can't be helped because he clutches and grabs.[3]

When we suffer a great blow, we find ourselves in inner chaos.

Like all the other certainties, God seems to disappear and to strain for assurances of his presence only makes us more aware of our desperation. Although I do not like feeling this, I have gradually learnt not to be too surprised. God is never there to order, though sometimes we become aware of him in ways we could not have expected. Once, in hospital, I plugged into my radio in the early hours and was reduced to tears by the words of an old pop song assuring me that someone was on my side and would take my part. Was God really the one throwing out his hand to reach me, lying down across the troubled water like a bridge? For that night and the following ones it was enough, as I juggled the stations hoping to hear the words again.

If you are looking in this book for some solution to the loneliness that pain and fear produce, or expect to read that I have learnt how to escape them, then I must disappoint you. But I have come to realize that these uncomfortable feelings are not wrong or a sign of my failure as a person. Whenever I am faced with a recurrence, or a new treatment, I go through the same sense of shock and helplessness and the same questions come back to be picked over once more. Some years after my first encounter with cancer, I find this entry. It could have been written at any time in these years: *I have a tiny lump – probably nothing, but it is there. I have to return in six weeks. I have vague pains in my right side, is it my liver? Do I tell the doctor now or wait for the next appointment? I am afraid. I don't want to die. I don't want to be sick. That's it really – I don't want to die, but if I must, I certainly don't want the indignity and loss of personhood of illness!* That lump faded away, the odd pains were no doubt caused by anxiety or indigestion. But the fact of cancer has changed my perspective. I dare not discount minor symptoms.

None of this gets any easier, but what has changed over the years is that I am beginning to understand that my feelings are healthy. I do not like them but I understand that they are a measure of my wish to survive and are God-given. Understood like that, they become bearable, no longer suggesting that I am without faith or that God has failed me. That does not mean I do not need sympathy and support; I am not proud of being turned into a quivering wreck when waiting for results, but that is the reality. Through the experience of cancer, some of the fantasy images of myself as *super-vicar-woman* have gone. What I am being asked to do is to accept my humanity, to understand that being afraid is acceptable to God. And so, when I remember, also to me.

Mary Craig has written about the subject of suffering, out of her experience of a son, Paul, being born with gargoylism, and her own work with survivors of Nazi concentration camps:

> Suffering is difficult to define. Basically, it is something (maybe quite minor) which happens against our will, is un-pleasant, and blows our carefully-regulated lives asunder. We protest, kicking and screaming, for the restoration of the *status quo ante*. If we can persuade ourselves to stop struggling and come to terms with the pain, adapt our natural rhythms to it, accept it as no better and no worse than it is, we may still be floundering in darkness, but the darkness may contain the promise of light. It is a paradox, but one that has been borne out again and again by indi-vidual experience, that it is *only* in the darkness, the empti-ness and hopelessness that we find our true selves.[4]

Mary Craig is not suggesting that enduring tragedy is good for us, but that the painful experiences that shatter our normal complacency *can* be creative. I take comfort from the fact that creation is sometimes a very slow process!

So cancer has meant for me an ongoing process of discovery and re-evaluation. I still go through the same reactions at any threat, but very gradually I have found it easier to accept that I do. Since my first illness in 1986 the disease has recurred several times, initially reappearing in lymph nodes four years after my first illness. At first only isolated nodes were removed but finally all the remaining ones were taken out. Then in

1995 my lower back became painful. I went to a chiropractor, thinking little of the pain as backache is such a common complaint, but the situation gradually worsened until I was in excruciating agony. Eventually it was discovered that the breast cancer had spread to my spine and one vertebra was in a state of near collapse. An emergency operation stabilized the spine with metal scaffolding, but the cancer remains in other bones, at present being kept under control by drugs. Throughout the years there have been false alarms, struggles for information, muddles and battles with the medical profession. Gradually I have learnt to argue and question and am confident with my present care. I am still learning and have to remind myself that doctors are not omniscient and that this is *my* life and I have to take responsibility. I am not a victim and must be prepared to speak out. But it is hard to ask for something to be checked again and risk being labelled a nuisance or neurotic woman.

When life is going well, we enjoy the pleasant illusion that we are in control of our circumstances and can predict what we shall be doing tomorrow and next month. In theory we acknowledge that at any moment a car crash or tornado could change our lives forever, that every breath is a gift, but we find it hard to believe. We tend to think of the Beatitudes as soothing, beautiful words that speak hope and comfort to people of any faith, or none: 'Blessed are the poor in spirit . . . those who mourn . . . those who are persecuted for righteousness sake . . .'[5] But these are no comfortable platitudes. On the contrary they challenge our complacency, as well as offering real encouragement in bad times. Of course we *do* know our need of God and that we are held in life, minute by minute; but *living* in that knowledge is the work of the saints and mystics. The Abbé de Tourville, a nineteenth-century French priest, lived in retirement from his early forties because of his poor health. His *Letters of Direction* written during his inactivity and decline speak with profound authority:

God gradually takes away our supports, whether of nature or of grace. With the passing of time we are apt to become more aware of the menace of finding ourselves left alone. What resource do you suppose there is, save that of making up our minds to put ourselves completely and delightedly into the hands of God? That is what we must do, casting a glance of absolute confidence towards Him: a confidence founded solely on His goodness. Do not argue with Him. Tell Him frankly that all your fears will not frighten, nor all your unworthiness intimidate you, when it comes to trusting Him; that in spite of everything, you do trust Him and, moreover, with peace, serenity, and love, both in season and out of season.[6]

I do not pretend to be able to echo the Abbé de Tourville. My own placing of myself into God's hand is more likely to be with a howl of pain and retracted as soon as the immediate threat is past. But I struggle towards his vision of what our lives should be; sometimes angrily, sometimes in despair. Somewhere I do know that God holds it all and that this knowing is where I begin my journey towards some sort of peace.

Whose Fault Is It Anyway?

After the shock of being diagnosed with cancer began to subside, I hoped to recover my equilibrium and return to normality. But although I steadily regained strength and energy over the following months, I found that recovering my confidence was a different matter. I felt that I could no longer rely unthinkingly on my body or my determination, or on God. Accusing questions reverberated in my mind: who was to blame for this? Was it God? Was it me? Was it the devil?

During my childhood and youth, although I never seriously doubted his existence, the fact of God seemed to have little or nothing to do with me. I was brought up to go to church and the Christian story had always made sense at a rational level. But it was only when I returned to church in my twenties, after a lapse of several years, that I discovered that God could be more than a vague concept. By this time I was married and the mother of two young sons. George and I had met when he came to London in 1967 to explore his British roots. His father was an engineer and had moved the family from Scotland to Zimbabwe (then Southern Rhodesia) after the war, when George was three. George worked for an insurance company and his passion was for rugby and sun-soaked African spaces; he was only in Britain for a working holiday. I was an idealistic art student, who loved poetry and English winters and dreamed of romance in a garret. Inevitably we fell in love and married! Neither of us belonged to a church at the time, although we had both been taken as children. Five years later, having insisted on the baptism of our sons for no reason that I could articulate, I was prompted to give church another try. I hoped that this time it might seem relevant.

By chance I arrived at an evangelical church and was intrigued to be invited to a Bible study meeting with other young mothers. Evidently my new friends read their Bibles regularly, expected to find what they read helpful and believed that God was involved in their lives. It seemed very strange to me and slightly scary, but certainly not dull. I had never come across an evangelical and had no concept of what the term meant; now I learned that Christianity is not primarily about trying to be kind or moral, as I had thought, but glimpsing that God bridges the gap between us and him. This was not a sudden emotional experience, although I read about life-changing conversions and longed for such glowing certainty. Instead I remained full of doubts and feelings of inadequacy, unsure that God could accept me despite my new friends' assurances that he could. But over the months I began, very tentatively, to trust that God might be interested in my difficulties and hopes. I started to pray and to read the Bible and slowly found that God was beginning to become real for me.

Two years later, George underwent a dramatic Paul of Tarsus-style conversion, leaving me jealous of his brimming joy and confidence, but wholly elated. Within another two and a half years we had moved to Salisbury for him to train at theological college for the ordained ministry. I expected that during his training I would be given some pointers about becoming a model vicar's wife. The church which had nurtured my faith had strong views about the position of wives as the secondary partners in a marriage and I had assumed these attitudes were an inevitable part of becoming a *real* Christian. The college had more liberal ideas and it soon became clear that my notions of sharing George's ministry, as an unofficial curate, were unrealistic. What I was seeking was a role for myself and I needed to explore the possibility. The following year I began my own training to become a deaconess (the professional role open to women before they were permitted to be ordained as deacons and priests in the Church of England). It felt like a wonderful gift; a second chance to study without the teenage angst of 'Who am I?' and 'Will anyone ever love *me*?' George's conversion from antagonistic agnostic to fledgling vicar had seemed miraculous and had transformed our relationship. Having married young, we had been in some danger of repenting at leisure. Now we had a shared foundation and began to learn to communicate with each other. We were excited about our hopes and dreams for the future, expecting God to lead us in our lives and ministries and attempting to trust him. There were various crises as we started college life and tried to work out where we were to go next, and we seemed to be constantly moving house and settling into new surroundings; but although this caused conflict and upset, it was also exhilarating. We did not expect God to smooth every path, but we assumed that if we sincerely and faithfully tried to serve him, we could depend on his care to 'work all things for our good.'[1] Cancer challenged that basic assumption.

Diagnosis had come at a time of enormous stress and upheaval. My mother had died the previous spring, my first experience of personal bereavement. I was shocked at the intensity of my grief and my preoccupation with death. She was not young and had been ailing for some months but, faced with her loss and with the reality of death, I was badly shaken. As well as this, George was unhappy in the parish and desperate to move on. It was his first post as vicar, which meant we had felt more settled after theological college and his years in the assistant role of curate. Now the church had fallen foul of the village worthies for suggesting that a wooden screen, commemorating those who died in the Great War, be repositioned. It was a storm in a teacup, the sort of thing that comes up regularly in the press, but George was made the target for abuse. There were notices posted in shops and articles in the local press and he felt unsupported by the church members who had initially encouraged the proposal. During the previous year, I had been appointed university chaplain and loved the stimulus and involvement with the students. A move would not need to affect my job, but I found it heartbreaking to uproot the family once more from the home we loved.

Through all of this I had struggled to keep hold of the notion that God was in control; that even when we failed, or made wrong or unwise decisions, God could overrule to bring about his purpose in our lives. This was central to the way in which I saw the world and to a great extent still is, but perhaps now the canvas seems larger and more complex. At the time I felt that I had to be strong for everyone, to hide my grief over my mother's death and my misgivings about our proposed move. Cancer was the final straw. What was I to make of this? Was it God's will, what he intended for me, some sort of test of faith? Was it my fault, the outworking of some sin or spiritual failing? Was it my inability to deal with the tensions in my life, my body's protest at the strain of the previous months? Or was it beyond God's control altogether? Was God rather less involved and interested than I thought? Or was I under attack from the devil? But if Satan was attacking, why was God not defending me? These seemed to be the options as I endeavoured to make some sense of the situation.

When something shattering happens to us, we have to review our ideas of how the world works and our place in the scheme of things. It is as if death, divorce or depression explodes in our lives, like a boisterous child upsetting a difficult jigsaw in frustrated rage. We are left with a scattered mess when there had been an ordered pattern. Some of the pieces may not have fitted too well, but now they are upside down on the floor! After the initial shock, comes anger. My first reaction was to blame God, and then myself. 'Why has this happened? Why has God allowed it?' I have heard people comment on the question 'Why me?' with the response 'Why *not* me?', and if we do not expect God to intervene in the world, this is a sensible reaction. But I spent my life encouraging people to believe that God is concerned about every detail of our existence. Much of my work was with students, reassuring them as they faced university life, or their first failed love affair, that God *cares*. If that is true, then 'Why me?' *is* the question. I continued to tell others that God would not let them down. But secretly I felt that he had, I felt abandoned.

Of course much of the world's suffering is the fault of human failing. On a grand scale our selfishness and greed leads to war and oppression and, in the lives of individuals, to broken relationships and isolation. Theoretically, I accepted that we live in a world in which there is a degree of randomness, having no answer for the undeserved suffering of accident, famine, or epidemic. But now, as someone for whom there was no answer, I protested. Why had God not changed things for me? I was his friend, wasn't I, on his side? He could do miracles, heal people, change lives; what was so wrong with me that he refused to help? Why didn't he take the cancer away, if he loved me so much? The shock was receding. My struggle was to establish in my own mind who was responsible for the situation. Was cancer my fault or God's? Was I living out the consequence of my behaviour or emotional life, was I being targeted or punished, or was something else going on? In terms of a bereavement process, I was moving from numbness to feelings of outrage, and the urgent need to understand. The questioning has continued over the years as I seek a coherent framework for the way I look at the world. My world now includes cancer.

Although I had not realized it until I was ill, I had always made a distinction between the way I thought about my own life and that of others; my personal world and the world of accident and natural disaster. I had all sorts of theories and sensible ideas for other people, but kept my own life in quite a different category. Now cancer meant that the division had broken down; I was one of *them*, the unfortunates to whom bad things happened. It caused a total revision of my previous assumptions about life. As I recovered from the first operation and radiotherapy the questions began to surface. I wrote in my journal: *I am now ready to take up the reins and continue my life, but internally I am in chaos. How has this happened to*

me? Was I neurotic and stressed, yes – so therefore to blame?
Was I nursing unconfessed bitterness and unforgiveness
towards those I feel have wounded me? Possibly, probably –
but no, not unconfessed. What am I to believe for the future?
Will the cancer come back? And if so, what will that mean?
George keeps saying, 'It won't come back. Put it behind you.'
That makes me feel that to think about cancer is wanting it to
return. But it is not easy to dismiss these months, to forget –
and if I can't, is that my fault too? What is going on? Is God
in control at all?

Although I was surrounded by love and support my questions were endless and unanswerable. George took the brunt
of them. He was wonderfully patient, hugging me, consoling
me, holding me at night, telling me it was all right to feel as I
did. However, he is not superhuman and the strain told on our
relationship. He constantly repeated that he was sure the
cancer would never return. At the time I could not see that his
own need to believe that I was cured was driving his attempts
to reassure me and reacted angrily to his apparent certainty:
'How do you know the cancer won't come back? What do you
mean you *know*?' George's way of dealing with a difficulty is
to ignore it until absolutely necessary, on the grounds that it
might not happen. Mine is to worry away at every aspect like
a dog with a bone, in order to be prepared for every possible
eventuality. Neither is wrong, but they are different and
inevitably this led to tears, misunderstanding and recrimination. Driven by my obsessive worrying, he would accuse me of
wanting to be ill. I would retaliate that he was callous and
uncaring. Somehow the rows also seemed to be my fault, the
guilt surfaced naturally!

For underlying my question 'Why me?' was a sense of condemnation. I wanted to blame God, but that was risky: the
alternative was to blame myself. At a deep level, I felt that
I was being disciplined or even punished by God. Was my
picture of a loving God accurate, or had I missed something?
Does God *will* evil, as he appears to do at times in the Old
Testament? I had rejected this concept as belonging to a

people of a different age and culture and at variance with the much stronger counter-emphasis in scripture on God as good and loving. So then was God testing me? If so I was failing the test dismally! Or was the devil to blame?

At the time I was asking these questions, I was in touch with a number of Christians who had an active belief in the malicious interference of demons in our lives. This offered a neat rationale for suffering and theoretically a solution: prayer for deliverance in the name of Jesus. For a time I was influenced by their views, but following through the belief that the devil is directly responsible for all sorts of accident and tragedy also seemed to make him far too important. I reasoned that although God has evidently allowed evil to be present and active in the world, the idea of a personal devil manipulating events in opposition to God's will makes nonsense of God as God. Surely God is more powerful than any devil. In my own case, I also found it unhelpful to see cancer as attributable to the devil's influence; wasn't my life given over into God's hands? Although I received prayer ministry for deliverance, I found it traumatic and unhelpful; my fears were unallayed and my questions unsatisfied. Dismissing the devil as the direct cause of my illness, I was left with the likelihood that the responsibility was mine! I am not describing sensible or rational arguments, but the muddle of panic and guilt that possessed me. I was quite unable to distinguish between my confused emotions and what I thought and believed to be true. Because of my tumultuous feelings, I did not know what I believed.

It is not surprising that I struggled with guilt. As the youngest child, by over five years, I had always felt the odd one out. My brother and sister were close in age, born early in the war years, before my father was sent out to Burma with the British army. I was born in 1947, after his return. For my mother, the experience of the intervening years had been pivotal. She changed, from an easy-going young woman who loved dancing and music, to an impatient and determined martinet. We children adored and feared her in equal parts. I wanted to be as strong and sure as she appeared, but I also watched other mothers and longed to be able to climb on her lap for a cuddle. I yearned for her reassurance but I was afraid to share my fear that I did not belong. As the only one that my father really knew in early years, I became very much his special child. To an extent, I think that my birth helped him to make sense of his war-time experiences and my unquestioning affection compensated for my mother's metamorphosis.

Not that I blamed her. From my earliest years I felt I understood her frustration. She grew up between the world wars in middle-class ease in a home with two live-in maids and a mother who loved to socialize. The post-war years were very different. She found herself frequently exhausted and at the end of her tether and blamed me, the late unexpected child, for her inability to cope. She was quite open about this, confiding in me from my early childhood, as I was often her companion left at home. At a rational level I understood her difficulties, but they left me with feelings of guilt and a deep lack of self worth. My father was my delight and my hero, but he worked long hours at the other end of the tube line and I saw little of him during the week.

Both my parents were high principled people, trying hard to do what was right. Both, I think, were lonely and longing for love. They struggled with the still rigid roles for men and women and with their relationship. Mother was active, vigorous and ambitious for us, particularly my brother. Father was gentle and passive, a quiet scholar, who hid behind the newspaper in the frequent eruptions. The tensions between them were evident. I felt that I was the cause: the extra one who was too much work for her, the favoured one who caused jealousy. I admired her, but felt rejected and undermined by her proud preference for boys. I loved my father, but he was often absent and sometimes withdrawn and remote.

Sent to a highly competitive and academic school, I under-achieved, acting the rebel and scraping through, until I discovered that I was good at painting. At last I felt that I had found something for myself and dreamed of creative fulfilment and fame. I studied painting at Chelsea School of Art, relishing student life and finally managing the transition from awkward teenager to apparently confident young woman. At the end of the four years I hit reality; being a student could not go on indefinitely, now I was expected to become an adult. In panic I fled into an early marriage and motherhood. I was not ready to face the world, or think about a career, and domesticity appeared to offer an escape. Underneath my bouncy exterior, I lacked confidence and yearned for approval.

Now when others seemed to suggest, subtly or not, that I was in some way to blame for developing cancer, I was hurt. At one level I protested vigorously, though at a deeper one I agreed. Hadn't I always been to blame? A burden for my mother and a cause of jealousy. I answered the question 'Why me?' with the ringing condemnation, 'Because you deserve it! It would have been better if you had never been born.' Somehow, somewhere, I must have brought this horror on myself. God is good, so the fault must lie with me. And yet I was outraged by this logic and everything in me protested my innocence. Of course I was a sinner, but how was I to blame for this? My reasoning was being driven by the unresolved guilt and self-doubt from my past; these were the real demons. I thought I had laid them to rest in the intervening years of adult life and moving into ministry, but cancer raised them to triumphant life in me. So I played endless mind games, compulsively attempting to discover an answer, or to make the answer come out differently.

Despite all this introspection and self-pity, I was not constantly sunk in gloom and recrimination. My energy returned quite quickly after treatment and we moved into the university chaplain's house, as George took up posts at the local hospice and at the university alongside me. I found I liked living close to the campus and threw myself unreservedly into my job, which continued to excite and challenge me. But intermittently the questions would surface. A chance remark or medical query could trigger them, so could a row, a book, a sermon or an introspective afternoon. I needed to ask the questions of myself, even though for the most part they seemed pointlessly destructive.

As I faced my own questions, I began to understand that all my life I had unthinkingly blamed others for their misfortunes. I had been brought up with the attitude that a healthy mind means a healthy body; that if a person lives sensibly and moderately, with due concern for others, they will escape any great tragedy. In my parents' home there had always been a veiled criticism of the sick and judgment was mixed with pity: 'Well, of course, she does much too much . . .'; 'He's a worrier, you see . . .'; 'What do they expect when . . .?' There was an assumption that when disasters occurred, victims must in some way have brought it upon themselves; not a consciously constructed theory about suffering, but an underlying way of looking at the world. So if a child was born disabled, I would wonder what trauma had occurred during the pregnancy to influence his or her development. When there was illness, I would shake my head over the stress, hidden anger, or loneliness that was being expressed physically. An accident might indicate a desire for escape.

I did not mean to be cruel; I was not stupid but, in trying to rationalize the tragedies of others, I had fallen into the trap of making easy judgments. I have since found that such reactions are common. Deluding ourselves that we understand the reasons for a tragedy gives a sense of being in control and helps us to disassociate from the pain of others. We can justify God and ourselves, while keeping a safe distance. Unconsciously we put ourselves into the position of the Pharisee in Jesus' parable. 'God, I thank you that I am not like other people,' he prays, listing the benefits and achievements of his life. Intent on reassuring ourselves that we are safe from similar disaster, we forget that it is the tax collector whose attitude is commended by Christ. In contrast to the righteous Pharisee, he is an outsider, despised for his collaboration with the occupying Romans, yet this man prays the prayer that has become probably more imitated than any other: 'God, be merciful to me a sinner!'[2]

I am sure that people were not aware of the distress they caused me when they made judgments about my situation, suggesting that I needed counselling for my hidden anger, or that I was over anxious, or attention-seeking, or had a secret fear of cancer that had resulted in disease. I do not mean that there is no possible link between mental and spiritual well-being and physical health; I was certainly under pressure when I was first ill and still grieving my mother's death. But it is too simplistic to link circumstances and sickness directly; the connections are complex and all sorts of factors, known and unknown, are in play. The full cause of any sickness or tragedy lie beyond our limited perceptions and we do well to refrain from making judgments of others or of ourselves. If we have no pains and problems we can be thankful. Our best prayer echoes that of the tax collector – 'Be merciful to me, a sinner.'

Over the years I have battled with my own neurotic guilt and self-condemnation. I have tried to be honest with myself about possible causes, fears and secret sins, and talked at length with the few people that I felt could help. Finally I have concluded that my circumstances and personality have been only a part of the reason for cancer, perhaps a minor part. It is true I am a driven high-achiever. I have difficulty expressing my emotions, or revealing any weakness or pain. I have a tendency to dismiss or reject my body. I fear rejection. I do not easily let go of past hurts and am frequently insecure, obsessive and fearful of the future. But I am also generally positive and outgoing; I was good at my work at the university and later working in the Vocations Department of the diocese, and enjoyed it tremendously. I am an enthusiast and I love life. I have everything to live for. Our marriage is loving and reasonably stable; I adore our sons and we see them regularly. I am extremely happy where we now live and feel loved and appreciated by the community. I have a sense of humour and even on occasions a sense of proportion. It seems there are at least as many positive factors in my life as negative. There are many people who live with stress or depression, or who have suffered cruelly from broken relationships or childhood deprivation, but *who are not physically ill.* I do not deny that I am at least as screwed up with life as the next person, but unless and until God shows me differently, I will not believe that I brought this disease upon myself or, indeed, that I am responsible for its continuing hold on my life. Numerous influences affect us in all sorts of ways, from the damage caused by the environment to our genetic make-up. I cannot take the blame. It is too great a weight to carry, but it is a continuing battle for me to resist the guilt.

In fact, newly-published research into the subject has found no correlation between attitudes and survival rates. A report published in *The Lancet* in 1999 by the Institute of Cancer Research and quoted in *The Times* newspaper claimed that 'women with a fighting spirit were no more likely to survive breast cancer than those with a fatalistic attitude,' and commented: 'These findings take the pressure off cancer-sufferers who often feel forced into becoming unnaturally optimistic.' The report continued: 'Researchers have also debunked the notion that breast cancer was linked to stress. The belief that the onset of cancer is linked to a stressful experience such as bereavement or extreme overwork goes back as far as the early eighteenth century, according to a report in the British Medical Journal.' I only wish such reports had been available fourteen years ago; they might have saved me some heartache. On the other hand my own attitudes, like those who proffered their opinions, were deeply ingrained and would no doubt have still taken time and effort to change.

I remember vividly a talk on a retreat. The priest was called Michael and told of his childhood and coming late home from school after a fight, grazed, dirty and with torn clothes. 'Mum, Michael's back,' recited his sister triumphantly, the strict family rule being that fighting was not allowed in any circumstances. Filled with trepidation, he waited for his mother to appear. Then came her reaction: 'Oh Michael, you've hurt yourself!' – and the embracing warmth of her arms around him. This picture of God is the strongest and truest for me now; a God who welcomes without question, a God who understands completely. Harold Kushner is an American rabbi whose son suffered from a disease called progeria, which brings about extremely rapid ageing and caused the boy's death at the age of fourteen. Kushner writes persuasively and lovingly of God as the champion and defender of the oppressed and troubled:

> Bad things do happen to good people in this world, but it is not God who wills it. God would like people to get what they deserve in life, but he cannot always arrange it.[3]

We are not responsible for the terrible things that happen, not to blame. And when we feel that we have been let down by life, the least helpful thing that we can hear is that this is our own doing. Even if there is a degree of truth in the assertion, does it *help* someone to feel the condemnation of others as well as having to bear their own pain and fear? And if we are blessed with peculiar perception and wisdom, there is little point in sharing our insights. Loving silence and tears, the gift of 'weeping with those who weep',[4] are infinitely more helpful. Sympathetic listening and hugs have done most to ease the burden.

The film, *Good Will Hunting*, tells the story of a young man who is at the same time a maths genius and a hoodlum. He works as a janitor, spending his spare time raising hell, until his gift is discovered by a professor in the maths department. Following his latest brush with the law, Will has to agree to study with the professor and also to see a therapist, in order to be released on bail. Will defies and ridicules the first counsellors that he sees, before meeting his match in the odd-ball Robin Williams character finally assigned to him. The relationship that develops between the tough, brilliant youth and the eccentric counsellor is the heart of the film. The therapist, grieving the death of his wife, allows Will to see his own hurt, as well as challenging him about the cost and meaning of love. Gradually an uneasy trust develops between them. However, Will remains well-defended, unable to risk exposing his own vulnerability. Then one day the therapist opens the file that shows photos of the injuries Will had suffered as a child, the bruises and wheals from his step-father's beatings. 'All this – it wasn't your fault, you know,' he tells Will. 'No, I know,' says Will. 'No, you don't. It's not your fault!' Will ducks his head, backing against the wall: 'I know that.' 'You didn't hear me. It was not your fault,' continues the therapist. 'Yeah. I know.' 'No, you don't know. Listen – it wasn't your fault! It was not your fault. None of this was your fault. It's not your fault. Not your fault.' The voice goes on insistently until Will breaks down in tears. At last he has heard. Sometimes, like Will, we need to hear it over and over again. The things that have damaged us, crushed us, and baffled us are not our fault. Of course we are responsible for our thoughts and actions, our malice and our wrongdoings. But the circumstances of our childhood, and the blows that come, are not our doing or our dues. They are *not your fault*.

I have needed endless kindness and the opportunity to tell the story, express my anger and grief and to ask the questions. There have been comparatively few people who have proved safe enough to really talk to. I have needed to know that they could cope with my blasphemies and distress, to be sure they will not judge me for anything I might say, that they will really listen and hear me. Best of all have been those like my spiritual director, Reg, prepared to confess their own confusion. I had come to know Reg some years before I had cancer, initially as a counsellor. He knew my background and my tendency to guilt and self-hatred and allowed me to pour out my grief and confusion now. 'It's a battle we all have to fight alone,' he assured me. 'No one can do it for you, we can only stand with you. Don't think what you *should* think or feel – only what you *do*, and let Jesus meet you in that.'

Early on, I knew that I could trust Reg with my questions, when he admitted that he had no answers. It helped so much more than those who seemed to have them all. After one visit to see him, I wrote: *Reg spoke of having prayed for a long*

period for a woman friend with cancer. He said he felt that he
and others had done everything; they prayed through all the
possible hurts that might have caused it, fasted, supported
her, held regular communion services, anointed her with oil,
they did everything right. The tumour went away almost to
nothing. Then it came back and she died in six weeks. 'I feel I
know less about healing than when I started,' he said. 'I am
like you, wanting to believe and not knowing what is going
on. It's a mess. It breaks my heart.' We talked about Christ's
'Why?' on the cross, and that even he had to die without hear-
ing an answer. That, and the welcome I had received when I
arrived, helped me through one bad patch.

Plotting a staggering course between the mine fields of cause
and effect, God and the devil, took me a number of years.
Naturally I looked to the Bible to help me and found that it
offered support and encouragement, as well as confusing and
sometimes contradictory suggestions about the reasons for
trouble and tragedy. As the various biblical authors explored
the question over several centuries, different theories about
the responsibility for evil and misfortune were propounded or
emphasized. The book of Job describes Satan as causing Job's
horrible afflictions, albeit as a test and with God's permission;
whereas in Isaiah, God declares: 'I form light and create darkness, I make weal and create woe; I the Lord do all these
things.[5] Similarly Hosea comments 'Come, let us return to the
Lord; for it is *he* who has torn, and he will heal us.'[6]

Jesus avoids being drawn on the question of blame. In
John's Gospel, when asked why a man was born blind, he
responds: 'Neither the man nor his parents sinned; he was
born blind so that God's works might be revealed in him.'[7]
This refuted the then current idea that misfortune resulted
from sin, either committed personally, even before birth, or by
someone in a previous generation. Instead, Jesus focusses on
how God might make use of the situation and work to bring
good out of suffering. In the Synoptic Gospels, Jesus does
attribute a variety of illnesses to the influence of evil spirits.[8] It
remains an open question whether he believed in demons him-

self or simply worked within the contemporary belief system in order to heal most effectively. In the West we have been less and less likely to attribute disease to demonic influence as medical science has progressed. Only a very few Christians want to treat physical problems with a ministry of deliverance today and such practices are usually reserved for diseases we cannot yet explain or control effectively.

It is clear in the Gospels that Jesus sees sickness as ultimately evil and alien to God's will for people's lives, a part of the destructive work of 'the enemy'.[9] Paul certainly claims that his unspecified disability comes from the devil, although he maintains that the responsibility for it emerging in his life rests with God: 'Therefore, to keep me from being too elated, a thorn was given me in the flesh, a messenger of Satan to torment me.'[10] It is interesting that Paul says that he repeatedly asked to be relieved of this problem, without any result, and only reached his conclusion about the purpose of this affliction as it continued to trouble him. I find it encouraging that he obviously puzzled over the question too. But apart from this one exception, Paul describes his difficulties, including imprisonment, beatings, shipwreck, hunger and thirst, as 'sharing in Christ's suffering'.[11] Similarly, in the first letter attributed to Peter, we are exhorted 'do not be surprised at the fiery ordeal that is taking place among you . . . But rejoice insofar as you are sharing in Christ's sufferings.'[12] The biblical view seems to be that although bad things are not generally specifically willed by God, all things remain within his control and may be a part of his larger purpose.

At various times I have found particular passages of scripture enormously helpful. Predictably these have often been the prophets' insistence on the durability of God's love: Jeremiah's: 'I have loved you with an everlasting love,'[13] and second Isaiah's: 'Because you are precious in my sight, and honoured, and I love you.'[14] As well as these comforting words, the suggestion that there is a purpose, or something to be gained from difficulties, has encouraged me tremendously. Hosea uses the idea of the Valley of Achor, which means the

Valley of *Trouble*, and recalls an episode when a particular
family were slaughtered there for their disobedience as an
image of renewal: 'Therefore, I will now allure her, and bring
her into the wilderness, and speak tenderly to her . . . and
make the Valley of Achor a door of hope.'[15] The psalmist
employs a similar picture when speaking of 'those whose
strength is in you . . . As they go through the valley of Baca
(weeping or drought) they make it a place of springs.'[16] There
have been moments too when verses that have no particular
reference to suffering have suddenly struck me as peculiarly
appropriate; like the bog-standard Evensong when someone
read out: 'It is the bread that the Lord has given you to eat.'[17]
The rest of the service passed me by, as I pondered whether
interpreting my situation as 'the bread the Lord has given'
denoted a mature acceptance or a negative resignation.
Whichever it was, it *felt* like a message of encouragement. For
that evening and many days following, the words seemed both
positive and helpful, as if God was gently urging me to stop
whingeing and get on with it, that the only way to make sense
of cancer was to see it as his way of dealing with me. All of
which brought me back to Mother Julian's reminder:

> He did not say, 'You shall not be tempest tossed, you shall
> not be work-weary, you shall not be discomforted.' But he
> said, 'You shall not be overcome.' God wants us to heed
> these words so that we shall always be strong in trust, both
> in sorrow and in joy.[18]

I was comforted and strengthened by the scriptures and the
writings of Christians through the centuries *and*, at the same
time, I continued to search for answers and for reassurance
that cancer was not my fault. My eventual conclusions about
the question 'Why' ended up somewhere close to where I had
begun. The universe is complicated and answers hard to come
by; there appears to be a high degree of randomness; we cling
to a belief that God both knows and cares about our situation
despite appearances to the contrary; we need to ask the

questions; no satisfactory answers are guaranteed. Not the answers, but the route by which I arrived at these unstartling conclusions was the important thing. My questioning was my way of working through the long period of anger and depression that followed the onset of illness and I discovered much about myself on the way. To some extent the ground has to be reworked whenever my medical situation changes. Although I never wanted to embark on this journey of self-examination, I am grateful now for having made it and even for having to make it again periodically.

We struggle with a world that does not fit our expectations of a loving God. We wrestle with the facts in an effort to justify God, forgetting that he can cope without our help. Perhaps in the end, if we need to blame somebody for our situation, the healthiest option is to blame God. He is used to taking the blame for things, this is after all *his* creation. God has made a universe where pain, injustice and random cruelty are part of the fabric, they are therefore *his* problem. Individual suffering is not sent as a punishment, or trial, or to teach great truths, but it seems that pain is an inevitable part of life, and in that sense God is in it all. Could it be that he also bears the cost?

The rabbit stopped shrieking when they stooped over it, . . . the small head thrust and nestled against his arm, and it died . . .

He looked down at the little draggled body, his mouth shaking. 'Thibault,' he said, 'do you think there is a God at all? Whatever has come to me, I earned it. But what did this one do?'

Thibault nodded. 'I know,' he said. 'Only – I think God is in it too.' . . .

'Do you mean Calvary?'

Thibault shook his head. 'That was only a piece of it – the piece that we saw – in time. Like that.' He pointed to a fallen tree beside them, sawn through the middle. 'That dark ring there, it goes up and down the whole length of the tree. But you only see it where it is cut across. That is what Christ's life was; the bit of God that we saw . . . We think God is like that for ever. But not the pain. Not the agony at the last. We think that that stopped.'

Abelard looked at him . . . 'Then Thibault,' he said slowly, 'you think that all this,' he looked down at the little quiet body in his arms, 'all the pain of the world, was Christ's cross?'

'God's cross,' said Thibault. 'And it goes on.'[19]

3

The Cross at the
Centre of the Universe

For a good part of my life I found the crucifixion a real problem. As a child I was filled with guilt on Good Friday. *He* had suffered and somehow it was my fault. I found it repellent that God had punished Jesus for things that I and others had done. What sort of tyrant was this, who tortured and killed the best in order to satisfy some notion of justice? Why was the suffering of Jesus necessary in order to forgive the human race? The drift away from church in my late teens had much to do with these difficulties, but there was no one I felt I could ask about them. When I became an adult convert, similar questions re-emerged. The evangelical church I attended emphasized personal sin as well as personal salvation. With my background I needed no encouragement to feel sinful; the joy I was supposed to know as a Christian proved more elusive! Explanations and sessions of prayer did little to sort out my muddles; encountering a different perspective at theological college helped much more, as did conversations with Reg, the counsellor who became my spiritual director. Over the period of theological training it dawned on me: Jesus, hanging on the cross, *is* God, there is no division between the two. That is what we are trying to say when we call Christ 'the Son of God', or 'God the Son'. It is God, the one who made it all, who became a human being so that we could know him; and God, in the passion of Christ, allowed the evil of the world to destroy him. He carried it, bore it, there.

This gives no answer to the question of why suffering exists, but may help us to relate to God in our troubles. Discovering this perspective anew, in the situation of illness, was vital for me. My search for someone to blame for cancer was in fact a search for a way to God, now that things had gone badly wrong. But just as it had taken years for me to grasp the idea that God does not remain safely aloof, but is involved in the pain of his world, it now took many months to relate this understanding to my present situation. Slowly I began to believe that I was directing my turmoil at the right person; that God is both caught up in the world's agony and is the God beyond creation. He is in the suffering and remains holding it all, ultimately answerable for all that happens. There is a story that an admirer approached Otto Kreisler, the master cellist, and gushed 'I would give my life to play like you.' 'I did,' Kreisler replied. On the cross we see a God who 'did', the God who spends himself, as creative artists or parents instinctively sacrifice themselves for their work or their child.

In the Old Testament, the problem of why God allows injustice and suffering is tackled movingly in the book of Job. An unknown writer turned the story of Job, originally a folk tale, into the most famous attempt to solve the eternal dilemma of a good God in a terrible world. Tragedy after tragedy befalls Job, first the loss of his home and fortune, then the death of his children and finally the onset of an excruciating and repulsive disease. His friends offer conventional comfort; he obviously did something wrong and anyway he should not presume to question God. But Job is not satisfied and demands that God answer his charge of injustice. Thirty-two chapters later God finally speaks, but only with questions of his own: 'Where were you when I laid the foundation of the earth? Have you entered the storehouses of the snow? . . . Has the rain a father? . . . Is it by your wisdom that the hawk soars?'[1] There are four long chapters of challenge. God gives no other answer, no tidy explanation for the injustices of life, no satisfactory philosophical argument – but Job is content. God has shown himself, demonstrating that Job has been heard, it is enough. The book ends with God commending Job for his integrity and rewarding him, back in the folk tale, with restored health, wealth and happy family. We are left with no reason, no purpose in the world's mess, only the fact that Job knows that his complaint has been accepted. That is no small thing.

For most of us, finding someone who will hear us is vital when we are in distress. Like Job we need to know that we are heard. After a visit to see my spiritual director I wrote: *Reg urged me to shout at God if I need to: 'Tell him he's a bastard, tell him how you feel.' He explained that I need to acknowledge my feelings of outrage and take them to God, to face them fully. We talked about the possibility that there is, perhaps, some use God makes of suffering; a collective unconscious giving meaning to our individual pains. But basically I was heard. To say how it is and have my beastliness accepted means I am heard! Yes, I know God hears, but sometimes that has to be made real for me, made present. Is that what the body of Christ is about? Hearing each other, washing feet and bearing burdens?*

We shall not, cannot, find the answer to why disasters strike and horrific ills befall old and young alike, both the vicious and the innocent. But to know that our protest is heard and respected give us value and perhaps helps us to discover some meaning in our experience. The one or two trusted people, who listen to us without condemnation, offer a most precious gift. God listens with them and in them, whether they are aware of him or not. He listens too when we dare to speak out our questions into the silence.

There is a story that one day in Auschwitz, a group of Jews put God on trial. They charged him with cruelty and betrayal. Like Job, they found no consolation in the usual answers to the problem of evil and suffering in the midst of this current obscenity. They could find no excuse for God, no extenuating circumstances, so they found him guilty and presumably, worthy of death. The Rabbi pronounced the verdict. Then he looked up and said that the trial was over: it was time for the evening prayer.[2]

The idea of God sharing the questions and suffering with and for his people is hinted at in the prophets: 'For the hurt of my poor people I am hurt, I mourn, and dismay has taken hold of me,'[3] laments Jeremiah. Hosea uses the image of the loving husband, betrayed by his wife, to express God's anguish at the unfaithfulness of his people, and Isaiah writes: 'In all their distress, it was no messenger or angel but his presence that saved them; in his love and in his pity he redeemed them; he lifted them up and carried them all the days of old.'[4] The New Testament fleshes out this picture of a vulnerable God, literally, in the incarnation. Jesus of Nazareth, the wandering preacher, was revealed through his passion and resurrection as the one who takes the world's woe upon himself. John the Baptist called Jesus 'The Lamb of God – who *takes away* the sin of the world!'[5] When the nails were hammered into Jesus' hands and feet, we see a reaction of forgiveness and love: 'Father, forgive them, they know not what they do!'[6] Could it be that all our anger and bitterness, terror, inability to forgive and our self-hatred will meet the same response? This theme, of a God who bears the agony as well as the sin of the world, has found renewed emphasis in the work of theologians of the twentieth century:

> When God becomes man in Jesus of Nazareth, he not only enters into the finitude of man, but in his death on the cross, also enters into the situation of man's godforsakenness. In Jesus he does not die the death of a finite being, but the violent death of the criminal on the cross, the death of complete abandonment by God . . . He humbles himself and takes upon himself the eternal death of the godless and godforsaken, so that all the godless and godforsaken can experience communion with him.[7]

Of course, it is one thing to begin to glimpse that as a theological truth, quite another to connect what God shows us on the cross with our personal heartaches. As I was going through my training for ministry I had learned to allow Christ *in* to how I felt. A letter from Reg, written long before I was ill, speaks of the relationship between Christ's passion and our ability, or otherwise, to learn to accept ourselves:

I will do my best to make the cross clear, though I should say that all the theologians who ever were have not been able to do so! Its another one of those mysteries which are in every aspect of our faith . . . This is how I see the basic thread of it. God the Trinity created the universe. In it he put man who could have a personal relationship with him. As it was one of love, there was always the likelihood of it going wrong (as in every human relationship). It did. God's heart was broken as he saw the effect on his children. He was therefore driven to put the matter right.

As he created us to live in time, he had to act in time. That means that at one moment in history he came among us. In doing so, he (a) showed that he took responsibility for what had happened, and (b) he showed mankind in human form and in a single life, the agony of love which is his from the first.

When he came, he let mankind in its sin behave to him as mankind in its sin behaves. It did. He took to himself the suffering inflicted by mankind in those few years, as representing the suffering mankind has and is always inflicting on him. The way he dealt with it was to absorb it. Everything the venom of man could do to him, he accepted and bore, and in return he gave forgiveness and love. The sin could therefore go no further. It was stopped and ended in him. He showed that man could hate, reject, ridicule, spit on, flog, drive nails into him and do whatever they liked, what they could not do was to stop him loving them.

That means that the way into God's heart is open to everyone, sinners though we be. No sin is powerful enough to keep us out, because he wants to bear the sin of each of us and he wants us to be united with him. Every sin is forgivable. It's the only thing God can do in the circumstances if he wants the world redeemed and us at one with him in love! To cement this relationship when we come in repentance, he lives within us. There, within, is the closest relationship that can ever exist for us . . .

Is your problem that you cannot forgive yourself, or forgive those who have hurt or misunderstood or despised you? If so, then take Christ into these relationships. God must work within our sin, just as initially he had to work within humanity on earth.

I hope all this helps. Again I warn you not to examine yourself. Let Christ take possession of you and leave him to do his work. Why spend time questioning what you cannot understand of yourself, when the living God is within you and can be left to do the job?

Over a period of some years I had began to understand that I could be myself with God. However, despite all the help that I had had in the past, I did not seem to be able to relate these thoughts to cancer. Faced with illness, I discovered that my self-acceptance was very limited.

Looking back, I can see that much of my initial depression was a result of fatigue, as my body recovered from surgery or radiotherapy, or adjusted to drugs. But patience has never been one of my virtues, least of all with myself and I felt condemned when life became a struggle. My dread of a recurrence continued through the first two or three years of the disease. It might never return, but I searched for lumps obsessively, fearing the worst. Sometimes I would discover them with horror and a sort of triumph, only to be told: 'No, it's nothing, but come back again if you are worried.' It frightened me more that I sometimes welcomed the idea, with a mixture of terrified bravado and a shameful urge towards self-destruction: 'Why don't I die – come and make me die,' I wrote after one scare. My confidence in a continued, unthinking existence was gone. I felt like a mouse, released by the cat, but only to be hunted for sport; any moment the disease might pounce again. I was ashamed of this morbid fascination and my inability to leave the experience behind, and afraid that this might cause the cancer to reappear. On the surface I remained positive and cheerful, I was loving my work and had adjusted happily to moving into Coventry. But underlying my active life, the fear and despair were just below the surface.

Finally in 1990, it happened: *On Monday I felt I should do something about the little lump in my armpit. At the clinic they flapped, Tuesday I saw the surgeon, Wednesday came in for the op. Today, Friday, I hope to go home. I don't yet know if it is malignant or not, but I suppose it has to be the way they carried on. Today I feel calm and unconcerned, though on Monday I was furious. I have so dreaded this and felt that I couldn't bear going through it all again. But it is not so bad, at the moment. There is something I have heard or read about us all hanging on a thread in the dark – that there is no security really, only God. Today, I know it.*

But this euphoric calm did not last and the lump was confirmed as having been malignant. I underwent further radiotherapy and new drugs were added to the regime: *There seemed to be no one to really explain. A doctor with poor English told me that the new tablets will attack my liver: 'But not to worry, we can function with only 12% of a liver.' Oh goody, I thought, that's all I need. 'There is always hope,' she told me. 'Some people who look ill go on for years, others look well, like you – then there is some family trouble and "Pouf" they are gone.' Was she human? Who let her in? A sort of terrible panic has taken over. I feel hopeless, unable to face it or fight. No one helps much, they tell me to be positive and so I smile as usual. But inside I'm screaming – I'm lost, not dying or damned, but lost.*

Intermittently, over the years, I began to see that the Christ who had died so horribly was the one who could come close to me in my confusion and fear. Initially I was ashamed of my weakness and need and so tried to ignore or fight my feelings, rather than work *with* them. Only gradually have I come to

realize that I can invite the crucified God into the emotions
and questions provoked by cancer. We cannot avoid or escape
the negative parts of our personality, but we can share them
with God. Later I added in my journal: *I wonder if all my
despair and hopelessness is something that Jesus can cope
with and be in – with me? It does not frighten or defeat or
demoralize him, or make him impatient. I am confused and
afraid. I am very angry. I feel betrayed, attacked and
ambushed by life, or by death . . . whichever it is. I feel alone.
But there is nothing he does not share, nothing he is not in.
There is something about 'having confidence in me', to quote
the ghastly song, that I want to hang on to; believing that all
this messy world baffled Jesus too. I don't mean just in
Gethsemane, but that he pondered it, struggled with it all
through his life. That anyway is how it is for me, and I have to
be able to say that what I am and experience is authentic,
worthwhile and of some value, rather than wrong, or despicable.*

It is impossible for us to think about the crucifixion without
picturing an old master or a stained glass window or crucifix.
An horrific sight, that could never be included on the television news, has become a piece of art, sublime, mediocre or
tasteless; a symbol of protest or of piety. This means that it is
impossible for us now to enter the mindset of the first
Christians and get any sort of glimpse of how Christ's death
must have appeared to those believers, struggling to work out
who Jesus was and what his death and resurrection meant.
Although in the Roman world brutality and violence were
more commonplace and less repulsive than they are to us, the
notion of God's chosen one dying as a criminal was incon-
ceivably shocking and repellent:

'Alexamenos worships his God.' This is the inscription
under the oldest crucifix in existence: a sarcastic scribble
representing the Crucified with an ass's head, probably
from the third century, found on the Palatine, the imperial
residential district in Rome. It would be impossible to bring

out more clearly the fact that the message of the Crucified seemed anything but edifying, more like a bad joke . . . Crucifixion, he (Cicero) maintained was the most cruel and repulsive, the most horrible form of death penalty. Long after it was abolished by the Emperor Constantine, until into the fifth century, Christians hesitated to depict the suffering Jesus on the cross. To do this on a large scale became customary only in mediaeval Gothic.[8]

The message that the early church wanted to emphasize was that Christ is alive and death defeated. The resurrection vindicated Jesus as the triumphant Christ and offered the promise of eternal life to his followers: they certainly needed the encouragement! In the early centuries becoming a Christian was at best uncomfortable, at worst dangerous. It was not until long after the church was established as a powerful force that the day of Jesus' death was transformed into *Good* Friday and took its place in the Christian calendar for special observance. Understanding Christ's cross in a positive light is not easy and we still tend to think of it in terms of the disaster that took place before God shows his hand, the dark tragedy that contrasts with the joy of Easter. For the original disciples the cross posed real problems: could this Jesus really be the Messiah, if he had died in such a manner? Could suffering and death be God's plan, a vehicle for God's action in the world? Did the resurrection simply reverse the horror of the crucifixion, or was there more to be learned through Christ's agony?

Although the story of redemption is familiar to us, we too often have difficulty comprehending the cross, both individually and as a community. 'In Christ,' declares Paul 'God was reconciling the world to himself.'[9] We see the crucifixion as the central event in God's great purpose and rejoice in what it means for the world, but we tend to keep it well in the pages of history, thinking of it as over, a finished event. Usually, too, we understand the crucifixion as something that happened to Jesus, but not to God; forgetting that there can be no separation within the Trinity, there is only one God. In a sense the

cross was beyond or outside time, for whatever happened to
Christ also took place, *takes place,* in the heart of God. On the
cross we see our loving and merciful creator enter into the
situation of human suffering and embrace it; God's self-giving
is revealed for all time and on a cosmic scale.[10] Because of the
cross, whether we are lonely or confused, in intense distress,
physical pain, or despair, we are not alone. But it is one thing
to read the words and give mental assent, another for it to
touch us personally.

In 1943 a controversial series of radio plays was broadcast
in which the author, Dorothy L. Sayers, had fought hard for
her portrayal of Christ as a flesh and blood character, as well
as for a departure from seventeenth-century language, before
colloquial translations of scripture were commonplace. She
draws out the scene when Thomas is confronted by the risen
Christ, to make clear this exchange of God: good for evil, life
for death, light for darkness, healing for injury:

Jesus: Thomas, because you have seen me, you have
           believed. Blessed are they that have not seen, and
           yet have believed.

Peter: (*who has suddenly become aware of some appal-
           ling implications*):
           Master – when I disowned you – when we dis-
           believed and doubted you – when we failed and
           deserted and betrayed you – is that what we do to
           God?

Jesus: Yes, Peter.

James: Lord, when they mocked and insulted and spat
           upon you – when they flogged you – when they
           howled for your blood – when they nailed you to
           the cross and killed you – is that what we do to
           God?

Jesus: Yes, James.

John: Beloved, when you patiently suffered all things,
           and went down to death with all our sins heaped
           upon you – is that what God does for us?

Jesus: Yes, John. For you, and with you, and in you, when you are freely mine. For you are not slaves, but sons. Free to be false or faithful, free to reject or confess me, free to crucify God or be crucified with Him, sharing the shame and sorrow, and the bitter cross and the glory. They that die with me rise with me also, being one with me, as I and my Father are one.

John: This then is the meaning of the age-old sacrifice – the blood of the innocent for the sins of the world.[11]

'Is that what God does for us?' asked John in the radio play, as the magnitude and meaning of Christ's self-offering hit home. Jesus' reply hints at a greater possibility; that just as God shares in our pain, we might be allowed some share in Christ's passion. As I have explained, it was only gradually that I began to realize that God could share with me in the uncertainty of cancer. The more startling thought, that we might stand with Christ in his passion, was one that came much later in my journey. First, I had needed to ask the questions about whether God was both good and involved, and how I could discover him in my new situation. Only later did I begin to search for a purpose in the messiness.

As you will have gathered, in all my attempts to come to terms with cancer, my own vulnerability has been the hardest thing for me to handle. It is one thing to write or speak about fears and failings and quite another to have them exposed. I have discovered that there is a real difference between disclosing what I am like on *my* terms, in a talk or book, and feeling out of control, foolish or belittled. Any situation when our life is sabotaged does that to us, and learning to respect myself in weakness has been difficult for me. Even when I was young and fully fit, accepting my body did not come naturally to me. Having it examined, discussed and sometimes feeble has felt demeaning. But it is this experience that has brought the aspect of Christ's physical vulnerability on the cross into sharp focus. We need an incarnated God, one who has been flesh and blood and there are times when we need a God whose body has been violated. After one unpleasant set of tests, I wrote: *Last night I was angry, I lay in bed furious with Dr J., with all Drs, with all men, with God. You bastards, I wanted to scream, all secure in your suits and uniforms, you have violated me! How dare you do what you have done – slicing, dosing, poking and prodding. I hate you! This morning I see that I am with Christ in this: 'the world's vermin, nailed to the world's barn door', somebody has called him, and all suffering is united with his. And my anger? I know it is only (only!) my feelings and that the Dr wishes me well, but it is hard to be constantly discussed and exposed by these kindly, well-dressed men. I realize my feelings are inappropriate, but all I can do with my shame is to offer it, ask God to enter it, accept it or change it. I think that is a part of what the cross is for.*

The cross demonstrates in graphic terms the fact that God is in all creation, to be found in failure, cruelty and decay as well as beauty and growth; and he has taken full responsibility for it all. This means that I can be myself in whatever state or difficulty I find myself. God is the one being in the universe who will not judge me for my rage and depression. I cannot do worse to him than has already been done, he is the safe place when I am not fit for human company.

At the end of the last chapter I quoted from a novel by Helen Waddell, which retells the love story of Abelard and Heloise. Peter Abelard was a philosopher and teacher in twelfth-century France, whose brilliance and scholarship drew pupils from all over Europe. At that time any academic career was, of necessity, within the church, and celibacy, though not enforced, was expected in a teacher and cleric. Abelard was invited to tutor Heloise, an exceptionally intelligent and beautiful young woman, and they fell in love and embarked on a famously passionate affair. Fulbert, the uncle and guardian of Heloise, was scandalized when he discovered their liaison, and took his revenge. His servants broke into

Abelard's lodgings at night and castrated him. Abelard and Heloise each entered religious life, never to meet again. In this final passage from Waddell's book, Heloise is visiting a mutual friend, Gilles, who has just received a letter from Abelard. The author makes the point that, when we are in agony, another suffering alongside us is the greatest gift we can receive. Their misery does not answer the questions but makes our own pains more endurable, their vulnerability does not end my uncertainty but helps me to bear mine. The notion of God's vulnerability helps most of all:

'Tell me, Gilles. It will be quicker. I cannot bear to read it. Does he speak of me?'

He looked down at the letter, twisting it in his hands. 'Not yet,' he said, very low.

She got up quickly and crossed the room. . . standing there, struggling to control herself, she heard behind her a small stifled sound . . . He had his face to the wall . . . distorted with soundless weeping. . .

'Don't, Gilles. Beloved, you must not. You must not. Dear Gilles, it was only for a moment. It is over now. It does not hurt, now.' Suddenly she stopped and gazed at him, something like bewilderment in her eyes, and almost a catch of laughter in her voice. 'Gilles, did you hear what I said? I only said it to comfort you. But it has come true. I can bear it now, because – because of you.'

He was silent for a while, rubbing his eyes with his sleeve. 'Is that true, Heloise?'

'It is true. Though why it should be – why you must break your heart to comfort mine – '

He looked up, the old speculative gleam kindling in his eyes. 'Quius dolore plage nostra curata est: et lapsus nostros aliena ruina suscepit.' . . . They say that St Columban wrote it. They never use it now. 'By whose grief our wound was healed: by whose ruin our fall was stayed.' I wonder. Is that what men have asked of God?'[12]

4

Does God Heal?

Becoming ill with cancer challenged my hard-won belief that God loves and cares for me personally. I have explained that, after the initial shock, my anger and despair caused an ongoing search for reasons for what had happened. I blamed myself or I blamed God, who must ultimately be responsible for everything within his creation; and at the same time I wanted to run to God for comfort and for a solution.

Many who wanted to help me were confident that God could indeed solve things for me. They lovingly encouraged me to expect a miraculous cure, citing numerous biblical examples of God's intervention in the world. 'God is a rescuing God, he is committed to you and will not fail you,' they insisted. Theoretically, I agreed with them. The God of scripture and tradition has always been proclaimed a *saving* God and the Hebrew term for salvation includes the idea of putting right, bringing peace and wholeness – as well as that of rescue. Surely I could look to God to change the situation. I wanted to believe that I could be healed and was quite willing to receive prayer, but of course there was no way of knowing whether anything had happened except waiting to see if the cancer recurred. Once the initial radiotherapy was finished I looked and felt perfectly well, but there was still no *positive* way of knowing whether the cancer had gone for good.

That caused muddle enough for me. There is a more general confusion about what is meant by 'healing'. For the sake of clarity I shall differentiate between the terms *cure* and *healing* in this chapter, using the word *cure* to describe the relief of a physical condition, *healing* to denote the biblical concept of becoming whole. In this sense, although a healing might include the cure of an illness, the emphasis remains on the idea of spiritual growth; similarly a person might be cured of an ailment without finding peace or moving towards maturity.

Some who are involved in healing ministry insist that prayer should always be for healing rather than cure. They claim that God is less concerned about a physical cure taking place than bringing someone to wholeness. Consequently their prayer is that, whatever the physical condition, God will be at work bringing sick people into inner harmony. Even if these people remain ill, or their situation deteriorates, the argument runs that they are still being healed. Of course in our Christian life we do long to become increasingly whole, healed, less self-centred and more at peace. It is also true that we shall all lose our health and strength and eventually die, life on this earth is not our ultimate end. In this sense we can all agree that our spiritual well-being is the really important issue, it is our spiritual life that will last forever. But that does not mean that our pains and difficulties in this life are not important to God. Stressing the spiritual aspect of health and well-being, in contrast to a *mere* cure, offers a tempting solution to the problem of believing in a benevolent God in the face of tragedy and sickness. Praying for healing, as opposed to cure, can allow us to say that there are no failures, no puzzles, only people being healed *in* their continuing suffering and ultimately by their death. But I suspect that all this lets us and God off the hook rather too easily.

Despite the importance of spiritual growth, to contrast it with curing the sick seems to me to be neither biblical nor entirely honest. When people are ill, unless they are hypochondriacs, they want to be made well. Perhaps they ought to be more concerned about their relationship with God, but meanwhile they are in pain, or unable to walk, or afraid. If they pray and do not recover, they are left with a problem – or rather two problems: not only are they still suffering but God has apparently failed to answer their prayer. There is no avoiding these unpalatable facts. Attempting to do so by emphasizing the distinction between healing and cure risks falling into the trap of separating body and mind, matter and spirit; as if the physical world were not precious to God. But he loves it.

When people's lives are blasted by illness, I do not want to attempt to justify God by suggesting that they are growing spiritually. This may be indeed be happening, but they have still been devastated by their experience. Of course God and they may be able to make something of the situation, but nonetheless their life has been spoilt and limited by their physical condition. Nowhere in the Gospels does Jesus suggest that cure and healing are different, or comfort the sick with the assurance that they will gain spiritual benefit from their misfortune. Jesus did not deny the real evil of disease, disability or accident; instead he cured those who were ill. In most instances Jesus made no comment about the spiritual state of those who were sick and came to him for help. There are a few exceptions, for example when the paralysed man is told that his sins are forgiven, or when one of the ten lepers returns to give thanks.[1] But generally there is no record of the spiritual condition or subsequent behaviour of the huge majority of people cured by Jesus.

Making the sick well appears to have been a priority for Jesus and it was this that first attracted people to him. The biblical accounts suggest that all who asked were cured and some who did not ask.[2] Josephus the contemporary Jewish historian confirms that: 'there was also about this time Jesus, a wise man, if indeed we should call him a man; for he was a doer of marvellous deeds.' Occasionally Jesus seems hesitant to offer help,[3] and one instance in Mark's Gospel records 'he could do no deed of power there, except that he laid his hands on a few sick people and cured them. And he was amazed at their unbelief.'[4] But clearly Jesus had a remarkable ministry, curing conditions from paralysis to skin disease, blindness to raising the dead. Some were made well by touch, some by a word of command, and others when they were not even in his presence.[5]

Christians believe that Jesus brought a foretaste of God's kingdom to the earth. Praying 'Your kingdom come', we ask for God's rule to be established and the end of destruction and decay. So we are praying for justice between individuals and nations, for the end of corruption and cruelty and are pledging ourselves to these kingdom values. Although Jesus did much to relieve individual suffering, clearly he came with a wider mission. His teaching ministry focusses on right relationships and priorities: 'strive first for the kingdom of God and his righteousness.'[6] His message was not that we should pursue a physically healthy, comfortable and fulfilled life as the supreme goal of our existence, but he did not dismiss pain and sickness as insignificant.

Over the centuries, the church has tried to follow Christ's example to care for and cure the sick. But just as there are no simple causes for illness or misfortune, the reasons some people are cured and others not seem equally complex. We know that the body is a self-healing mechanism and will cure itself of minor ills and we accept that the intricate relationship of mind, spirit and emotions affects our physical well-being. We acknowledge that release from tension, or having a particular goal, can prolong life or even precipitate a spontaneous cure. Medicine and therapies of all sorts, orthodox and alternative, do much to cure sickness and alleviate symptoms. If we believe in God, we see all of this as God-given healing. The fact remains that Jesus made the sick well and told his followers to do the same. Some claim to have been made well by prayer, sometimes in spectacular and dramatic ways, but those who are miraculously cured by our prayer are in the minority. When it is me or mine that needs the cure, I want to know why, and if possible how to become someone who *is* cured. During the last forty years the practice of prayer and laying on of hands has become increasingly common in many churches. Occasionally horror stories are reported of false claims or emotional manipulation, but many assert that they have been helped or even cured by prayer. Although we may not expect wonders, we look to the Gospel records and we hope.

Bernadette was a priest who died of cancer at the age of 47. She believed in God's power to cure and heal and left a moving and honest account both of receiving healing and of coming to terms with death. I shall quote from her story in some detail, as it so clearly illustrates the complex threads of cure, healing and wholeness. These excerpts from her unpublished journal begin in a period early in 1994, when Bernadette had learned that cancer had returned, two years after initial diagnosis and treatment. She had been told that it was certain to prove fatal:

Looking back I realize that in those first few months I didn't hope and pray assertively for healing. I believed that I would do better than medically expected but I had accepted the prognosis of death in a way which later I understood to be fatalistic and resigned.

Bernadette was encouraged to attend a service of prayer for healing at Coventry Cathedral:

One felt encircled in prayer. When John prayed for me I found myself praying 'thy will be done, Lord'. At the end of the service John came and asked me whether I would like to come and talk to him . . . a conversation which became a turning point of my journey.

He asked me to tell him the story of my illness, which I did. He then said to me, 'Bernadette, you are preparing to die, and you mustn't. I have known other people who have been completely healed and you must believe that you can be well.'

I told John that I had been anxious to be prepared because of Rob and the children. But he assured me that I would be given time to prepare if and when that was needed.

I went away feeling very deeply stirred, not yet able to grasp the hope that I had been given . . . From that day onwards I experienced a quite new sensation in my body, a sort of energy – an adrenaline – which I can only believe was healing. That Sunday the resurrection joy of Easter was very real to me.

Bernadette realized that her mother's long periods of illness before her death, when Bernadette was still only nineteen, had had an impact on her attitude to life:

A part of myself had accepted the idea of death without a fight, even as a gentle exit from the struggle of life.

Just as my mother had been 'in love with easeful death', I must put any such thinking far away. This felt an almost physical act, as if I was shedding some skin. But it was not easily done.

Three months later Bernadette was on retreat:

One of the first talks she (the retreat leader) gave was on the importance of recognizing our wounds, which we bring from the whole of our lives, and realizing that, just as Jesus still bore his wounds in his resurrected body as part of his manifested glory, so we bear our wounds for the healing of others. We must believe that our wounds will be trans-formed to honours within the love of God.

She was invited to reflect on the story of Jesus raising the daughter of Jairus to life:[7]

As I pondered on that little girl, it struck me that she was thirteen years old when Jesus raised her to life, just the age I had been when my mother became ill. I realized also that with Mum's illness a part of me had died, certainly my childhood had died and all the joy and freedom of that childhood . . . he suggested that I should identify with the little girl and act out the story in the quiet of my own bed-room, so I took courage and did just that. As I did so I found that it was quite difficult to be 'raised to life'- something in me was still holding on to the 'easeful death'. But then I did get up and felt wonderfully refreshed and imagined myself going down to the lake to play with my friends – full of life and health.

Since then, the grief I have carried for so many years has gone and one day, after the retreat, I realized with a start that I had fallen in love with life and didn't want to let it go.

Bernadette had a year of good health before becoming ill again. On 11 October 1995, she wrote:

Between last night and this morning a truly wonderful change has happened in me. I no longer feel the frustrated fight, the realization that I am not getting better and a long-ing to be so . . . I feel a real peace, a sense of handing over into God's hands and that it is now possible to do that.

And five days later:

It is clear now that I have not got long to live and I have no fear of dying. In fact now that the time has come, I feel an impatience. I have fought the good fight as best I have known how. So I 'lay hold on life and it shall be thy joy and crown eternally'.

'All things work for good for those who love God.'[8]

Bernadette died peacefully on 20 October 1995. Through all this time God was at work, healing the part of her that had wanted to avoid life and in time bringing her to a great peace. Bernadette was not cured of her cancer but she did became more whole; in that sense she was indeed healed. I still want to protest at the premature ending of a life so full of joy, meaning and promise, as much for those left behind as for Bernadette herself. God did not plan for Bernadette to get sick in order to do her good, but with her co-operation he was able to bring her life on earth to completion. Regardless of our physical condition, we are all on a journey towards wholeness that extends beyond the limitations of this life. At one level, death, when it is inevitable, is no doubt a healing – we go to God. But that does not mean we can avoid grappling with the problem of sickness and untimely death.

Healing and wholeness focus on our spiritual, emotional and mental well-being and over the last century much has been discovered about the human mind, our unconscious motivations and the emotional turmoil that has its source in infancy and childhood. Despite the sometimes sharp differences between the various schools of psychotherapy, there is a core conviction that past experiences may cause difficulties in the present. Therapists and counsellors can help us to understand our feelings and to find strategies for change. Within the church, there have been those who have linked these insights to the Christian story and offer prayer ministry for *inner* healing. Some encourage inviting Christ to enter into and change old painful memories, sometimes with dramatic effect; in much the same way as Bernadette found her feelings about living changed as she meditated on the story of Jairus' daughter. Others, most notably Frank Lake, founder of the Clinical Theology Association, have attempted to go deeper, asking the Holy Spirit to work in the unconscious and bring unremembered hurts the surface. As with all forms of therapy, mistakes can be made and misguided or unsupervised individuals have sometimes done harm. But at its best, this approach can offer insights and resources that are truly healing. When proper support is provided, real breakthroughs can take place and many testify to the emotional and spiritual healing they have received:

When we allow ourselves to face and feel emotional pain in the love and power of Christ, its grip on us is broken and it can be used constructively to mellow and mature. We commonly meet those who are not able to allow the pain to be brought out because in earlier years they were not permitted to express themselves . . . The result of such situations is that a solid blockage is constructed which shuts off the areas needing release and healing. As we point this out, we may say something like this: 'Christ has seen your suffering, every bit of it from birth, and He has suffered with you. Now, if you will go back to it and feel it again, He can let you know that He has suffered for you and will now suffer with you. Let us take Him into the cold-shut-off parts within to bring His warmth, His loving acceptance, and His healing.'9

Discovering God's acceptance brings us to greater peace with ourselves, whether this comes about through counselling or psychotherapy, through prayer ministry, or as part of our spiritual growth and personal prayer life. There is a sense that this continuing journey towards integration and wholeness is far more significant than the cure of disease. It is a journey towards God that none of us can avoid and will presumably continue after this life is over. But there is no escape from the difficult questions about God's intervention on our behalf, or lack of it. Despite God's promise of sharing our pain and the invitation to a wholeness beyond the physical, the question is urgent and unchanged. Should I ask to be cured? 'Yes!' says the New Testament. Then if God does not make me well, can I be sure he still loves me? Does God intend good for me in every situation? Is there some great master plan for each of us, that includes the terrible things that happen? It is indeed a puzzle.

The questions became more complicated for me after cancer reappeared in 1990. Until then my struggle had been to believe that I *had* been cured, by a combination of medical treatment and the prayer of the church. Now I had to accept that apparently I had not, but still to continue to expect to be cured in the future. It felt like being asked to execute a double somersault. The fear and insecurity were heightened, as was the tension around hoping and praying for a cure. Trying to believe this was a possibility was now more difficult, but the need to do so more intense. I wrote in the following weeks: *Apparently someone has said 'Is it cowardice to hope?' For me the cowardice would be not to hope, but to give up. It seems to me a lot easier, hoping is the difficult thing. I feel I cannot bear the disappointments if the cancer keeps on coming back, if I get really ill, if I am to die. I am afraid of hoping. And is my hope supposed to be 'For this life only'?[10] as Paul puts it. There is some of me that longs for 'home', for heaven, and always has. C. S. Lewis always writes of heaven as home. Was he particularly holy then, to die in his early sixties? I mean did God deliberately choose him for heaven early, like handing out a gold star? Or has the healthy ninety-year-old got the key – does that prove good behaviour, or special favour with God? Or is it always: 'What is that to you? Follow me.'[11] Is it somehow trusting that God is in it whatever happens? That if I am cured, his victory has healed me and that if cancer overtakes me and I die – what? . . . I failed to have faith? I failed to live as he wants? I failed to face my inner conflicts? Or would it be that he has a purpose in it, and is taking me home? Is that a cop out? Should I say 'I WILL be well?' But I don't know. Certainly Christ shares it with me, I do know that much. As George said four years ago when I wept over my scarred breast: 'He was disfigured.' I do see now that he shares it. I had not realized then, that cancer is a chronic illness. I thought you either had it and died, or you didn't. But it is an ongoing progressive disease, with ups and downs – that's bad. But not as bad as being automatically fatal. I thought I wanted total health or death. I'll settle for the struggle after all, and struggle to believe that God knows and is in it all.*

I was no nearer to an answer to my questions and am not today. We speak of the mystery of God and of course, to atheist and agnostic, it *is* a cop out. But they do not seem to have any answers either. At one and the same time, we hold to a God who suffers in and with his creation and affirm that he is a God who saves and heals. We know that at times God intervenes to make people well and that he is always making whole.

The Bible asserts that there is an overall purpose and direction for creation. It begins with human beings living in

total harmony with each other and with God in the garden of
Eden, and ends with a vision of restored humanity in a new
heaven and a new earth: 'God himself will be with them; he
will wipe away every tear from their eyes. Death will be no
more; mourning and crying and pain will be no more.'[12]
Picture language perhaps, but the message is clear. God
intends to do something with the tangles and the tragedy of
human existence and will bring all things to a final harmo-
nious end. We believe that the cross is the moving force that is
bringing about this new creation, although we cannot see *how*
this process is to be completed. In our better moments we
glimpse the possibility that our own suffering might also have
some purpose; that our pains might in some way join with
Christ's passion and bear with him the agony of the world,
purge the sin, pay the price. Paul hints at this when he writes:
'I am completing what is lacking in Christ's afflictions for the
sake of his body, the church.'[13] We strain to grasp the thought,
wanting to understand and to see the full design, but in the
here and now it is hard to keep a sense of God's great purposes. When we are in trouble we struggle to believe that God
cares and is in it all, that 'even the hairs of your head are all
counted'.[14]

We are naturally driven to pray for those who are sick,
including ourselves, but have to contend with the muddle of
cure and partial cure, healing and death. We hope and pray
for God to act: sometimes it seems that he does, often it does
not. One way of putting it would be to say that God's intervention is frequently hidden from us, but that sounds danger-
ously complacent. We go on praying anyway, because there is
nothing else to do. Certainly answers come in ways we had
not imagined and we can be changed by prayer, whether our
own or that of others. I have great sympathy with the sceptic
who tells me that such consolations are nothing but a con-
venient fudge. On the other hand the conviction that there is
no rhyme, reason or answer to be found can be just as con-
venient. In my experience, to refuse to hope is not necessarily
a sign of facing reality.

Looking back, I understand that my initial reluctance to place much confidence in prayer was due to fear and to my need to deny the illness, rather than to optimism. Although I allowed others to pray for me, I was afraid to hope or expect to be cured. Similarly, I adopted a fatalistic attitude to my lifestyle: 'Cancer will get me, or not, and there's nothing I can do about it. I may as well continue as usual!' Often this kind of robust attitude is held up as an example of courage; for me it was about paralysing fear. I could not face the fact that I had cancer, so I tried to ignore it. A fatalism that denied me any responsibility in the situation was easier for me to handle. This was not bravery on my part but cowardice; it was also a necessary stage in my journey towards accepting my situation. At the time I was quite unable to face the implications of the disease and it would have been cruel and useless to confront me. I needed time to adjust, to absorb the initial shock and to begin to deal with my own questions. I had to make my journey at my own pace and in my own way. For no one else can make it for us, or even, at times, with us.

As the years have gone on, I have become more at ease with receiving healing prayer. I feel less responsibility for being cured and so have less fear that I will be blamed if cancer returns. Paradoxically, this is because the disease *has* continued to plague me. I have grown used to having cancer and to some extent have accepted its presence in my life and so have those who want to pray for me. Other people are less prone to give sweeping assurances of complete cure and this leaves me free to discover a level of expectation that is real for me. I do find it increasingly possible to believe that I am kept well, held in health, by the loving faith of others. Every month I receive prayer and laying on of hands and know that friends frequently pray for me in my absence and I am grateful. Feeling myself surrounded and soaked in prayer strengthens my faith and gives me a sense of being protected from the spread of the disease. This may be an illusion, but it feels good. For me it is easier to believe that loving thoughts and prayers can have a physical effect on my immune system than that visualizing *bad* cancer cells being destroyed by *good* fighting cells will keep me well. I am quite willing to accept that different techniques or methods of relaxation, massage or diet can have a similarly beneficial effect on others. If pushed, I would want to add that inviting God into the equation cannot but help; but exactly what happens when people pray is beyond me. Of course God hears, cares, is there. Beyond that I dare not go.

Sometimes the people who pray simply put hands on my head in silence, sometimes they use words or anoint me with oil. Sometimes I am prayed for by an individual who claims a particular gift of healing, at others by friends and strangers. Generally I receive prayer in the context of some sort of Christian service and I would be uncomfortable being prayed for by anyone outside the Judaeo-Christian tradition. But I do not think it is terribly important how they pray, or who they are, only that I am helped to know that God is working and to be open to whatever he is doing in me. I do believe that I am being healed in the sense of becoming more integrated, but imperceptibly. I know that this is God's ultimate intention for me and he generally seems to get his own way in the end.

I have also realized that I have a responsibility for my state of health, if not to receive a dramatic cure, at least to respect the degree of well-being that I do enjoy. Some time ago, on the phone to Dorothy, my 96-year-old cousin, she admonished as usual: 'Now don't do too much.' 'Well, I try,' I laughed, and was shocked at the vehemence of her response. 'You must not be so *selfish!*' she scolded, 'It would be very selfish of you to get over-tired, after all that George does to look after you.' This conversation was a real gift to me. We are so used to thinking of selfishness as *not* doing things for others, it had not occurred to me that it could be selfish to *do*. But then I remember that much of my activity is about fulfilling expectations and striving to be liked, and I know that Dorothy was right. The much harder thing for me, as it is for most of us, is to say. 'I'm sorry, I can't take that on.' And leave it there.

Two particular instances of receiving prayer stand out for me. The first took place in St Thomas's Hospital early in 1996. I had had surgery to my spine, replacing a vertebra damaged by cancer cells and supporting it with various bits of metal scaffolding. All had gone well, but as I had had intensive radiotherapy just prior to the operation, as well as a fair bashing to my innards during surgery, I was understandably nauseous. In fact I felt like death; I was quite helpless and unable to move. Now and again nurses turned me over for a short time, but the best thing in my life was an electric fan wafting a breeze in my face and helping to keep the nausea under control. Extremely sick and unable to attempt food, I lay as still as possible feeling very sorry for myself. Reading was too much effort, visitors exhausted me, and the nights were endless. I remember asking George if I would ever get better. Privately I found it hard to believe; I was so weak, dependent and demoralized. I wondered how I would bear the situation if, at some future time, I knew I could not recover. 'How do people endure dying, if this is what it is like?' Not that there would be any choice, of course. But I was aware that I clung pathetically to his repeated assurances that one day soon I would be able to eat again, that some day I would have the strength to move, to sit or stand or even walk. After eight days with no change, George brought a note from a friend in the parish: 'We had a day of prayer for you yesterday,' she wrote, 'so I know you will be feeling better by now.' 'Well, I'm not,' I remarked ungraciously, and tearfully asked George to pray for me. As soon as he touched me, it felt as though an electric current had passed through my body. The idea of resurrection power filled my mind and a sense of energy and life pulsing through me. I felt no less ill, the nausea remained, but I knew that I had turned a corner: 'I shall eat tomorrow,' I announced. This was literally a square inch of dry toast, tasting extremely nasty. But I was not sick and I continued to eat. It was quite clear that I had begun to recover from the surgery and that prayer had played a part in my recovery. It seemed that George's prayer had ridden on the back of all those offered in the parish, and brought me renewed vitality – resurrection.

Slowly and steadily I regained strength and nine months later was well enough for a treat. We had four days in Athens, and on our return journey Raymond sat down next to George on the plane. He was huge and gregarious, a dentist and part-time pastor of a Pentecostal church in San Francisco. Raymond began to talk to George about his ministry of healing, and how he had seen numerous miracles, including the paralysed restored and cancers disappear. Feeling rather irritated and decidedly cynical, I leant across and told him I had secondary cancer. Undaunted he produced a bottle of oil and a Bible. He gave me a short lecture on the instances of complete cures in the Bible, anointed me with oil and prayed. Encouragingly he also spoke about adequate rest and a suitable diet, all the helps that assist the immune system to function well. It was a bizarre experience, but not distressing or intrusive. I felt nothing, except a sort of satisfaction that all that could be done in the way of prayer had now surely been done. A plane over the Alps must cover everything, I mused. I need continual treatment to limit the ongoing damage to my skeleton, but at the moment the situation seems to be under control. Perhaps things would be worse, but for Raymond!

Over the years I have been prayed for in small groups, in hospitals, in church services, as well as in a few huge gatherings where people experienced the power of the Holy Spirit in dramatic ways. Whether I have been aware of God or not, being prayed for has felt good. The only occasions when I have been irritated or distressed were when the inexperienced, insensitive or over-confident have intruded on my space or freedom. This has occasionally happened, when someone has bounced up and announced that God has told them to cure me or offered a directive, usually of the 'Believe and receive your healing' variety. But these have been in the minority. Knowing that I am surrounded by the faithful prayer of the community strengthens and encourages me, giving me a sense of being loved and supported that is healing in itself. But the question of cure and healing remains a mystery. A letter from my spiritual director, speaking about the resurrection life, sums it up:

> In his life on earth before his death, Christ was still the resurrection. He was eternal life even though he had not demonstrated it to humanity. As such he moved among the greed, lust, cruelty, bewilderment etc. of mankind, while he lived and preached the resurrection life. Most could not see it. Both his resurrection life and the world's condition went on side by side and he affected a little bit of it. In his death he suffered the effect of sin/evil around him, but it could not overcome the resurrection life . . . The world of sin and evil did not annul the world of the resurrection life. It was and is there in its true reality. Even though sin and evil are to some extent still within the lives of those 'in the resurrection'.
>
> The frustrating problem of healing is but one part of all this. The resurrection breaks through sometimes and at other times it does not. The resurrection life is *still there*, but the 'world' is also there and we cannot know what goes on between the two. No one has fully answered this problem of sin/evil/suffering. We can only suffer and hope – and funnily, rejoice.

Sometimes, when we least expect it, people are cured of a physical condition (sometimes something different from what made them ask for prayer), or relieved of inner tension. I have not heard of anyone feeling worse for being prayed for, as long as there has been no suggestion that 'success' depends on their faith. I have heard of those with little or no belief in God receiving a cure and some uttering furious challenges heavenwards. God does answer our prayers for healing and cure, but remains *other*, and beyond our control. It seems that the particulars of why, when, and in what way he makes his presence known and felt are beyond us, and will remain so. God transcends all that we can dream, and is also God within, the life of all that lives.

5

Wholeness

Exploring the subject of cure and healing has been important for me. I want to go on living and to continue in relative health for as long as I can and I recognize that this is a healthy, God-given desire. I have also come to realize that my deepest need is for peace of mind. However, suggesting that I must just accept and 'come to terms', particularly early on, merely aggravated my distress. Learning to own the anger and turmoil has been part of a journey for me, but an important one. Not that I have now arrived at an euphoric state of peace; my acceptance of my situation and myself is always fleeting and intermittent, not to be relied on. But perhaps I find it easier to recognize that when I am tipped into fear by some worry about the disease, the inevitable emotional upheaval is just a part of the uncertainty, not a permanent state of mind. Confidence and peace are not constant, but perhaps they are slowly growing.

This painful groping towards peace and awareness of our need for inner tranquillity is common to all human beings, whatever our circumstances. We hope for relationships that satisfy and a lifestyle that offers freedom and fulfilment, we are aware that at a deep level we crave a satisfaction beyond the physical or material. So Soames, in *The Forsyte Saga*, rich, respected and successful, longs for 'more':

And only one thing really troubled him, sitting there – the melancholy craving in his heart – because the sun was like enchantment on his face and on the clouds and on the golden birch leaves, and the wind's rustle was so gentle, and

the yew tree green so dark, and the sickle of the moon pale
against the sky.

He might wish and wish and never get it – the beauty and
the loving in the world![1]

We yearn for healing in its deepest sense of becoming more
whole. But peace with ourselves is always elusive and requires
the willingness and ability to face ourselves, and to practice
honesty of this kind is costly. It will bring us to the source
of intimacy and beauty that we long for, it brings us to
God.

In order to recognize our true feelings and motivations,
we may need the help of others. Of course, exposing our
weaknesses and doubts is risky. It is hard to abandon our
masks of competence and cheerful equanimity and allow
ourselves to be seen as we are. Even if we know our listener
well, there is still the chance that *this* time what we have to say
will be too mean or grotesque, and meet with rejection. I am
always tempted to avoid the nub of the story, the precise truth,
or the naked need. But I have found that until I am prepared
to speak freely, I am often not really aware of my feelings or
motivation. We need to face the dark side of our nature to
discover who we are. As the little child is supposed to have
exclaimed: 'How do I know what I think, until I see what I
say?'

C. S. Lewis' book *Till We Have Faces* is a retelling of the
myth of Psyche and Cupid. In the original myth, beautiful
Psyche is loved and wooed by the god Cupid. Knowing his
own splendour is too great for mortal Psyche to bear, Cupid
hides himself from her, remaining unidentified and only
becoming visible in the dark of night. Psyche is in love with
Cupid and content to live in this way but, on a visit home, she
is goaded by her elder sisters to light a lamp and steal a look at
Cupid as he sleeps. A drop of hot oil wakes him and Psyche is
banished to undergo various taxing tasks before finally, after
surmounting all her trials, being reunited with Cupid and
becoming herself a goddess. In his book, C. S. Lewis recounts

the story from the point of view of Psyche's oldest sister, Orual. In his story, ugly Orual had cared for Psyche from birth with a passionate and possessive love and it is her jealousy of Psyche's joy in her lover that brings about the disaster. Orual lives out the remainder of her life in bitter regret for Psyche's loss, for she sees only as far as Psyche's banishment and the loss of her bliss with Cupid. Orual endures punishing loneliness and despair, refusing to face her own part in the tragedy and nursing bitter accusations against the cruelty of the gods. Only at the end of her life do the gods reveal to Orual that her own pain, struggles and recriminations have played a part in easing Psyche's trials. Loving Psyche as she does, even in her all-too-human and twisted fashion, she has shared in bearing Psyche's burdens. Her sufferings have lessened those forced on Psyche, without her ever knowing. But before this truth is shown to Orual, she has to face herself. She is required to bring her long complaint into the hearing of the gods themselves and to discover who she is.

There was utter silence all around me. And now for the first time I knew what I had been doing. While I was reading, it had, once and again, seemed strange to me that the reading took so long; for the book was a small one. Now I knew that I had been reading it over and over; perhaps a dozen times. I would have read it for ever, quick as I could, starting the first word again almost before the last word was out of my mouth, if the judge had not stopped me. And the voice I read it in was strange to my ears. There was given to me a certainty that this, at last, was my real voice.

There was silence in the dark assembly long enough for me to read my book out yet again. At last the judge spoke.

'Are you answered?' he said.

'Yes,' said I.

The complaint was the answer. To have heard myself making it was to be answered. Lightly men talk of saying what they mean . . . I saw well why the gods do not speak to us openly, why should they hear the babble that we think we mean? How can they meet us face to face till we have faces?[2]

Ultimately, facing ourselves brings us face to face with God, whether we recognize him or not. He is the unknown, yet well-known, listener to our secret horror, tears and yearnings; and in the end it is only God who can change our feelings about ourselves. Of course it helps if we feel secure about God's attitude towards us!

It took me a long time to understand that for most of my life I have had a split picture of God. On the one hand I believed that God was forgiving and generous, I saw Jesus' strength and compassion and knew that this must be what God is like. But there were also less positive pictures drawn from authority figures from my past who had made me feel dismissed or belittled. They too had contributed to my image of God and for years these fears made me suspicious of whether I could really be fully accepted by him. Gradually a truer picture of God has emerged, but it is still subject to misconceptions and confusion, as it is for all of us. We cannot understand ourselves and those closest to us, let alone our creator! But, at least we can come to see that God is big enough to accept all that we are. It is this realization that has done most to help me to accept myself.

I wrote in an earlier chapter that cancer exposed the fragility of my self-acceptance. Before I was ill, I thought I was much more *together*. Perhaps one of the great benefits of illness or trauma is that it forces us to be real about ourselves. My spiritual director was right to encourage me to speak out my reactions to the disease. I wanted to curse God, and needed permission to express my fear and fury and then to discover that God was not changed by them. All that I feel comes as no surprise to God. He knows it and I believe accepts me when I accuse him of injustice, charge him with indifference, or call him a cheat and a fake – before dissolving into tears. In the weeping, I realize that I am heard and that God looks with love. It is God who can gradually transform our misunderstandings, bitterness and lack of faith and move us towards wholeness. Our part is to actively co-operate with this transformation and a vital aspect of that is to begin to face God and ourselves.

There is a story of a man whose little daughter was very sick. On his way to the hospital one afternoon, he bought a huge and wonderful chocolate cake; not expecting her to be able to eat any, but in an attempt to cheer her. Perhaps he hoped to encourage her to want to go on living. He arrived to find that she had just died; he was too late. This father had prayed fervently for his daughter's recovery, often visiting the hospital chapel; now he went straight there and hurled the cake at the figure on the crucifix, pinioned to the wall. That was a profoundly faith-filled response, and one that we sense instinctively draws God's compassion rather than his condemnation. I am not suggesting that we decorate our local church with chocolate when things get too much for us, but in whatever way we can, we may load our anger and despair on Christ, the one who came to bear the sorrows of the world. In times of crisis it may indeed mean some symbolic act of violence and this will not be blasphemy. How else are we to react when our world falls apart, when we are bereaved or sick, when our families are torn apart, or we lose our self-respect? Far better to direct our rage at Christ, where it will be ended, than at ourselves or others where it can only cause further harm. We need to learn to pray. I do not mean spending time in intercession or prayer with others, good and worthwhile though these forms of prayer might be, but becoming intimate with God and facing him with a willingness to be known. Prayer then becomes a part of the process of being made more whole, of being 'engodded', held and transformed in the presence of God. There is no formula that will automatically do this. God works within each of us as an individual. As the Narnia books remind us: 'He is not a Tame Lion.'[3]

There are as many ways of praying as there are people, but the heart of praying is this knowing and being known. For me,

a routine is vital. I need a regular place free from distraction
and early in the day before my mind has begun to start organ-
izing the world. For others, being outside and using their eyes
and ears brings them into a vivid awareness of God. Some find
movement a help: exercise, walking or driving; some like to
use music, to work in the garden, to paint, knit or cook, using
the time to experience God's presence. For some there is an
ongoing conversation with God; some use the Bible in an
imaginative way, picturing themselves in the Gospel stories
and allowing Christ to speak to them or repeatedly savouring
as particular phrase or word; some write down their thoughts
and feelings 'before God'; some just sit. What is important is
to find a way of prayer that works. There is no right method,
only the longing for God. And the understanding, or the bold
hope, that he longs to be with us, that he is at work inside us.

I have found that consciously inviting Christ to be with me,
to see me and hear me at my worst, is an important part of my
prayer. I want to be quiet and at peace when I pray and try to
focus on God and dismiss irrelevant thoughts from my mind.
But at times of stress or fear, turbulent emotions surface
naturally. Forcing them down again or trying to ignore them
does not help. I need to voice them or write them or feel them
with God and my prayer has to be, 'This is where I am today;
Lord, be in this too.' Although this does not change my negative emotions, it helps me live through them. I do not banish
the darkness, but I can invite the light to enter and believe that
it comes; and over time, I am changed. It is not easy to remain
relaxed when deep feelings arise in prayer times and I have
had to learn that these are not barriers, but things that God
wants to challenge or change in order to bring me greater
wholeness. We are to bring all that we are to God, and not
concern ourselves with having the right sensations. An illus-
tration might help to explain what I mean.

When I was confirmed at the age of fourteen, I got very
worried about having the right feelings when I received communion. I thought of it as the one moment I could be forgiven
for all the failures of the previous week. If I did not get my feel-

ings right, I reasoned, I would not find peace. So I tried hard to have holy thoughts and became obsessed with *not* having wicked ones. At that time, the most sinful thought that I could imagine was the word 'penis'. I would nerve myself for the journey to the communion rail: 'I mustn't think it, I won't think it . . . *penis!*' Defeated again, I gave up on God for another week, and returned to my pew angry with myself and disappointed with God. Although this amuses me now, it was a real difficulty and, sadly, not one I felt I could discuss with my parents or the rector.

When I returned to the church as an adult, I had a similarly fraught attitude about taking the sacrament. 'Was I worthy? Would Christ come to me? Would I feel accepted?' Just as I had in my teenage years, I wanted reassurance in the form of a particular spiritual feeling and was regularly disappointed. It was not until I learned to receive holy communion as a discipline that I began to relax. Taking the bread and wine is an act of obedience. Because we are bidden to do so by Christ, we take and eat; that is all that is required and anything that happens as a result is God's affair, I can do nothing. Miraculously the sacrament received in this way becomes a gift, not necessarily an emotional or spiritual experience, but something of God that nourishes us, a vehicle for God. Just as I eat my lunch, without troubling about the process of digestion, I can ask Christ to enter into the way I am today, happy or sad, bored, lonely or resentful; holy feelings are not necessary. I take him in to my thoughts, emotions, memories and relationships, and every cell of my body; bit by bit, daily, hourly, God enters in. To put it another way, I gradually become more aware of the presence that has always been there, within, loving me into life.

After I discovered that I had cancer, it took me a considerable time to see that my reactions of outrage and loss were not beyond Christ's compassion or care. I was swamped with powerful emotions which I longed to escape and the last thing I wanted to do was to face my anger, guilt and fear. I did not understand that God seemed unreal and distant precisely *because* I was unwilling or unable to accept my feelings and be with God in them all. Instead I clung to the idea that, as someone who talked to others about prayer and God, I should be able to cope and punished myself for my weakness. This is still a mistake I can fall into.

In 1992, I wrote: *My real battle is with me, my anger and self-hatred, and there has been a lot of it, these last few months. I have shingles, which doesn't help the general low level of energy. We seem to row too often. I feel that I am saying 'Life is difficult for me, support me, encourage me,' and George hears a demand to do the impossible and make me better. Someone said yesterday, 'You are what you do, not what you say you believe.' That's really frightening. I speak so much meaningful claptrap and can be such a negative, self-pitying cow, particularly at the moment! I have been to see various people about my fear of cancer over these months: 'If I know more, I can be more responsible, feel more in control' – that syndrome. The Social Worker told me I could visit the Bristol Clinic, learn relaxation, and she would like to counsel me for my deep fears. I found her patronizing and scary. The Macmillan Nurse (Social Worker's recommendation) told me I should have a positive attitude, and that only the doctor could discuss my medical situation. I didn't really want to discuss it, I wanted to be allowed to say that I am afraid and don't know how to deal with the fear. The Cancer Support Group had a speaker on mind over matter, but there was no opportunity to share our feelings. I went to the GP, wanting him to give me permission to take some time off. He said I had post-viral fatigue, that it could easily become ME and that the only thing I could do is to keep going and not give in to it. I was furious. But in a way he helped. There is no support available from the medical end, then, and precious little understanding. Just more of the same – stiff upper lip, bright smile and keep right on to the end of the road!* Writing the journal has helped. I notice that often entries begin with anger or turmoil, some tale of misunderstanding or panic and end with resolution, at least temporarily. That does not mean I have solved the problem, but I arrive at a degree of peace, enough for the day. It has taken me years to realize that God does not judge me for my fear of disease and death, or for my self-pity, vanity and confusion. That in all things, he is *with* me, assuring me, like the prophet Ezekiel mourning with the exiles at the River Chebar: 'I sit where you sit.'[4]

Because an attempt to discover inner silence in prayer has helped me, I will write a little about it. Somewhere familiar and comfortable where I can relax works best for me. I usually light a candle and have some sort of image in front of me, an icon or postcard, anything that can serve as a starting point. I sit and look for a while, feet on the floor, head level, back straight to help me remain attentive. I begin by taking deep breaths and consciously relaxing muscles, feeling myself *here* and present in God's presence. Then I try to enter into inner quiet, aware of God who is always within us and all around. It is this focus on God that I want to develop. Even for a short time each day, it takes effort and concentration; it also offers immense benefits. Along the way I have needed huge helpings of encouragement and this letter from my spiritual director is typical:

> As regards prayer, you are experiencing what we all experience. You must just keep going on, knowing that most of the time God will not seem near, and being very grateful when he does give you a taste of his presence. All the mystics tell us that if we always want the 'consolations', then we are being babies in prayer. Your problems of wandering thoughts, lack of concentration etc. are everybody's problems and only years of patient plodding on will overcome them. All you experience is right and normal – it's all 'just beyond'.

So gradually I have learnt not to be disturbed or surprised by my mind reliving yesterday's conversation or planning for tomorrow. I keep a note pad by me for things I *have* to remember and a journal for the deeper feelings and thoughts that come. Often I do not use the journal, but sometimes I discover my emotions only as I become still and, if they are disturbing, I set them down. Then I bring God into that part of me too. My intention is continually to bring the focus back to God, knowing that the less *I* do, the more still I shall become. And God, *thou*, the one who is, looks back at me with love. A repeated phrase or single word helps to quieten my chattering thoughts: 'Jesus', 'Lord', or the traditional prayer of the Eastern Orthodox church, and Luke's publican: 'Lord Jesus Christ, Son of God, have mercy on me a sinner.' The writings of the mystics have been a great encouragement, especially when packaged in short bites. Mother Julian of Norwich, with her astonishing vision of God's warmth and approval, is irresistible. I can use words like these to chew on, returning to them when my attention has drifted again:

Peace and love are always alive in us, but we are not always alive to peace and love.

God says: 'I love you, and you love me, and our love shall never be broken.'

He loves us and enjoys us, and so he wills that we love him and enjoy him, and firmly trust him and all shall be well.[5]

When I began to pray in this way, I was aware of a nagging sensation that I had experienced something like this before. It took some time before I remembered sessions in Art Galleries as a student, gazing and gazing at a particular painting, learning to look. The prayer of silence feels very much the same sort of process. Spending time with this God who feels our hurts, I can discard the pretences that fool the rest of the world and learn that I am accepted. I am not far along the road and I doubt that many of us will travel a huge distance in this life. Mercifully God is on our side, and will bring us to where he wants us in his own time, even if it takes an eternity to do it.

If we have any sort of faith, we believe that there is a purpose and direction in creation. Without it, our existence is meaningless. With some faith in God, however flickering and fitful, we struggle towards an idea of being renewed. If God wills all of creation to be brought into harmony and joy, then our part is to co-operate and allow him to make us increasingly whole. The Bible talks about us becoming like God: 'when he is revealed, we will be like him, for we will see him as he is.'[6] Sometimes people have the impression that this means becoming plaster saints, but God has made us to be unique. Becoming Christ-like means becoming fully ourselves; we lose our lives in order to be remade and find our true identity.

Of course becoming whole, perfect, will not be completed in our lifetime. But we can make a start by allowing ourselves to be seen by God as we are. Naturally we fear that if we show our true selves, we will meet with rejection. We realize that for the most part we are petty, vindictive and mean-spirited and dread being exposed to uncreated purity and light. Surely such perfection will unmake us! But the reverse is true. Just as the love of God is revealed in a broken figure on the cross; our brokenness, however despicable in our eyes, meets only love. An overwhelming love that makes us whole.

Sitting here with God (I suppose that is what I am doing) I realize that I am bored with my endless self-preoccupation. I don't think I have ever felt that before – shame, Barbara, shame! But I am aware that I want to be different, freed from myself. Do I mean that? It sounds grand and pious! I have been re-reading Till We Have Faces. *One thing comes clear, we cannot know God face to face till we have faces ourselves. That is, until we know our own true selves. There's a line in the book: 'Die before you die. There is no chance afterwards.'[7] Death will not be an escape from self-pity, depression or loneliness, I have to leave them here and now. Then, I suppose, neither life nor death need frighten me. I see that self-pity has been my comfort blanket, a secret luxury for years, particularly the last one: 'I have cancer and no one cares. I am blamed for cancer and it is unfair. If things go against me, I will die of cancer.' Nauseating stuff. 'Die before you die.' If I were to lose myself, lose my selfish preoccupation with me – then life and death would be immaterial, not my business, not in my hands. I have a long way to go!*

Orual, having read her complaint at the unfairness and cruelty of life, finds that she is required to stand before the gods and hear their judgment. She is about to discover that she too can be made perfect:

'We must go to your true judges now. I am to bring you there.'

'My judges?'

'Why, yes, child. The gods have been accused by you. Now it's their turn.'

'I cannot hope for mercy.'

'Infinite hopes – and fears – may both be yours. Be sure that, whatever else you get, you will not get justice.'

'Are the gods not just?'

'Oh no, child. What would become of us if they were? But come and see.'[8]

6

Is There Any Meaning in All of This?

Each mortal thing does one thing and the same;
Selves – goes itself; myself it speaks and spells,
Crying *What I do is me: for that I came.*[1]

Hopkins' wonderful words of exultation and confidence
express the joy of simply being alive. I love to bellow them
under huge cloud-swept skies, or savour them quietly at
moments of high achievement. They represent a shout of
affirmation for the created world. As a child I grew used to the
notion that I had potential, which usually meant that I was
considered bright but lazy! Middle age came on me with a
shock, not so much for loss of looks or vigour, but because I
realized that potential was no longer enough. Suddenly solid
achievements were expected. Ageing, illness or tragedy force
us to acknowledge that dreams may not come to fruition, or
may come too late for us personally. The *rightness* of the
world, that we revel in when life is full and happy, deserts us.
We begin to wonder how we fit into the scheme of things, or
even if there is a 'scheme of things' at all.

I remember wandering round Oxford one January afternoon some years ago, during a break in a conference which I
was co-leading. There must have been something about the
winter streets and the warm light from the windows that took
me back to youthful dreams of the future. Suddenly I realized
with a shock that all those long-cherished fantasies of being
the ideal mother-figure, warm and unflappable, casual but
efficient, were now out of date. It was too late now for that
vision. There had been no red-flagged Victorian kitchen reek-

ing of new-baked bread and my children were nearly grown up. I was not consciously mourning the approaching end of family life and we had had some happy family years in several twentieth-century homes, but I wept. That particular idealized image of myself no longer made any sense, even as fantasy. I mourned not so much the loss of my children's childhood years, but what the fantasy had represented; that particular unrealistic idea of myself and the sense of limitless possibilities, of a wide open future. Without them I felt suddenly lost.

The pictures we have of our future dissolve and refocus continually. Most of the time we hardly notice them changing. Wild dreams of success adapt to the present job and fantasies of perfect relationships turn to hopes for grandchildren, or opportunities for travel. But bereavement, sickness or a sudden change of circumstances brings us up short. We are confronted with the truth that all we possess is the present moment, and that may be all we are going to get. Of course this is true every day of our lives, but we seldom realize or acknowledge the fact. It does not make us comfortable. Along with the shattering experience of a personal tragedy, we are forced to face the unpalatable truth; everything is changed and cherished plans may no longer be attainable. We struggle with a loss of purpose and of meaning.

As I indicated earlier, there are stages in any grieving process. Most of us experience shock and may know some guilt and anger in the pain of coming to terms with our loss and arriving at an eventual acceptance of the new situation. The questions that I faced about the cause of my illness, who was to blame and whether or not God had sent it, gradually gave way to others. Over a period of years, and particularly once I had suffered a recurrence, my questions changed. I worried less about why I had cancer and began instead to ask what I could do with and in the situation. To some extent I had begun to accept what had happened.

In time those who are bereaved generally move on from their initial state of shock and denial to a period of acute awareness of their loss. This can take the form of a painful depression or feelings of endlessly searching for their loved one. As I began to let go of the urgency of the question 'Why?', I became aware that I needed to find a way forward, that I was now involved in a different search. Looking back, this seemed to parallel the searching that can take place in the grieving process. It was as if the emotional landscape changed, the familiar landmarks and signposts had disappeared and I was constantly trying to find my way.

I realized, once the cancer had come back, that whereas I had hoped for lengthening periods between check-ups and eventual discharge, this was not going to happen. There would always now be hospital appointments, drugs and tests. As time has gone on there have been various operations and treatments and some tiredness and pain. I can live with the situation, I have no choice; but I have had to work out how I am to think about my life as it included these things. Is there something I can make of cancer beyond constantly harping on regrets? Having lost my image of myself as outgoing and full of energy, I have had to find out about a new me, the one who has to ration her vitality, who needs personal space and looks forward to a more limited future.

Victor Frankl was an Austrian psychiatrist, a Jew, imprisoned in the concentration camps during the war. His parents, wife and brother all died. Out of his experience of unimaginable suffering, injustice and oppression, Frankl came to a conviction of the crucial importance of 'meaning' for human life and health:

> I became disgusted with the state of affairs which compelled me daily, hourly, to think only of such trivial things (the next scrap of bread, chance for some rest or warmth) . . . suddenly I saw myself on the platform . . . giving a lecture on the psychology of the concentration camp! All that oppressed me at that moment became objective, seen and described from the remote viewpoint of science. By this method I succeeded somehow in rising above the situation, above the suffering of the moment.

. . . any attempt to restore a man's inner strength in the camp had first to succeed in showing him some future goal. Nietzsche's words, 'He who has a *why* to live for can bear with almost any *how*' could be the guiding motto for all psychotherapeutic and psychohygienic efforts regarding prisoners. [2]

And not only prisoners. For any who are struck down by calamity, or whose circumstances are just plain bloody, the belief that there is some purpose in it all can get us through. Even when things are going well in our lives, the fear that there is no ultimate meaning to our existence, or no future worth having, can drive us in a search for pleasure and distraction. When we meet with suffering, particularly when it is unexpected or unjust, our failure to find any reasons for what is happening tantalizes us endlessly. After the war Frankl continued to explore and develop his ideas about our need for meaning, eventually creating his own theory of psychotherapy, which he named logotherapy. Frankl devoted the remainder of his life to practising and teaching his principles, convinced that to find meaning in our situation is the key to fulfilment:

> It is one of the basic tenets of logotherapy that man's main concern is not to gain pleasure or to avoid pain but rather to see a meaning in his life. That is why a man is even ready to suffer, on the condition, to be sure, that his suffering has a meaning.[3]

The holocaust has incomparable significance for our generation. In all the technological advances, the slaughter of those millions stands as a terrible reminder of the depths of human evil. For many, the holocaust is their greatest barrier to faith: how could a good God allow cruelty and destruction on such a scale, and moreover to the people most peculiarly his own for four thousand years? Many feel that, because of the holocaust, their personal difficulties cannot even be categorized as suffering, that the holocaust has forever defined the meaning of the term, and that any pains we face are not worthy of the name, suffering. There *is* no comparison. I have no conception of enduring hatred and cruelty, of starvation and brutality, murder or genocide. For this reason, I have looked to some of the survivors for their answers: their experience, of all the peoples of the world, may offer hope.

And what of human ideals, or of the beauty of innocence or the weight of injustice? And what of God in all that?

I didn't understand, though I wanted to. Ask any survivor and you will hear the same thing: above all, we tried to understand. Why all these deaths? What was the point of the death factory? How to account for the demented mind that devised this black hole of history called Birkenau?

Perhaps there is nothing to understand.

Was it the will to testify – and therefore the need to survive – that helped pull me through? Did I survive in order to combat forgetting? . . .

If anything motivated me, it was my father's presence. In the camp we were close, closer than ever, we thought we might be the last survivors of our family . . . We depended on each other: he needed me as I needed him. Because of him, I had to live; because of me, he tried not to die. So long as I still lived, he knew he was useful, perhaps even indispensable. In my eyes, he was the same man, the same father, he had always been. If I was gone, he would lose his role, his authority, his identity. And conversely: Without him my life would have neither meaning nor goal.[4]

So Elie Weisel, winner of the Nobel Peace Prize, describes his survival of Auschwitz and Buchenwold. It was his relationship with his father that kept him alive, just as for Frankl his ideas of a life's work gave him the will to live. Frankl cites these two motivations in life, the need for meaningful occupation and for love, as fundamental to us. He also speaks of one other driving force. The experience of the death camps, as well as our individual comparatively minor sufferings, demand a purpose *in* the calamity. As well as finding a way to survive, we need to be able to make something of the experience itself. Frankl insists that this too is possible, that to be put in a situation of difficulty and pain can *give* us meaning:

> Most important, however, is the third avenue to meaning in life: even the helpless victim of a hopeless situation, facing a fate he cannot change, may rise above himself, may grow beyond himself, and by so doing change himself. He may change a personal tragedy into a triumph.

> When a man finds that it is his destiny to suffer, he will have to accept his suffering as his task; his single and unique task ... His unique opportunity lies in the way in which he bears his burden.[5]

We are all engaged in a struggle to discover meaning, although we may succeed in avoiding the search for years at a time. Mostly our achievements or personal relationships give purpose and joy, through them we have a sense of value and our lives make sense. We focus on a particular goal for our lives: career, home, financial security, or family, and are surprised to find ourselves suddenly uneasy or let down when the work is completed. Immediately, we cast around for a new focus to give meaning to our lives. But when we are confronted with suffering of some description, everything is transformed. Now we are faced directly with the question: 'What meaning is there in life itself?' It is not a bad thing to wrestle with these thoughts, but it is painful. Frankl and those like him who drew meaning from the cataclysmic suffering of the holocaust encourage us to believe that if we can find purpose in our worst experiences, we shall be the richer for life.

Christians naturally look to the cross as the key to discovering purpose in suffering and, over the centuries, theologians have sought to interpret Christ's passion in ways that engage with human experience. The twentieth-century holocaust offered a new challenge. Are there ways in which this man-made hell can throw light on the agony of Christ, or the purposes and nature of God? Or can the fact of the cross give significance to the obscenity of the death camps?

It must also be said that, like the cross of Christ, even Auschwitz is in God himself. Even Auschwitz is taken up into the grief of the Father, the surrender of the Son and the power of the Spirit . . . God in Auschwitz and Auschwitz in the crucified God – that is the real basis for hope which both embraces and overcomes the world, and the ground for a love which is stronger than death and can sustain death. It is the ground for living with the terror of history and the end of history, and nevertheless remaining in love and meeting what comes in openness for God's future. It is the ground for living and bearing guilt and sorrow for the future of man in God.[6]

At a personal level the cross may appear to complicate the situation for us. If Christ suffered so much *more* than anyone else, are we allowed to complain at all? To be told to look to the cross for consolation and meaning can leave us feeling baffled and inadequate. It took time for me to glimpse that Christ's pain might be able to give meaning to mine. I still work at it, grow confused, forget and come back again. Writing in 1991, not long after cancer had first recurred, I asked: *Jesus was called a man with authority. He healed and preached, did miracles and told the clergy where to get off. So did he change? When we see him as the suffering servant, the patient Lamb of God, are we saying that events get too much for him? Or did he decide, or discover, that there is greater power in powerlessness? It sounds good but does it mean anything? Or is that so much holy drivel, the usual Christian excuse when we don't have an answer? Did Jesus think he offered his life for love? Did he think about it at all, did he expect his arrest or was it a shock? Did he welcome the cross, or just accept it, will it, or suffer it? Did he happen to it, or it*

[handwritten margin note, left side:] Could this help the Jews who did not believe in Jesus –

[handwritten note, bottom:] I believe Jesus gave his life — he did not take it. He never had got away!

to him? We see Jesus as in control, in contrast to our own helplessness. Well, if he was, then it was easier for him to deal with the agony, not harder. If he knew that he had a purpose and willed it, then it was bearable, I think. Maybe, like me, he just knew it had to be. I knew I had to discuss bowels yesterday, no big deal you would think, but I didn't know there would be a student there and how humiliated I would feel. I mind the kindly carelessness that doesn't acknowledge my nakedness, the feeling of being caught in the headlights like a rabbit. And yet I know that I collude with it by pretending I don't mind, by making light remarks and underplaying my worries. Is there any relationship with Christ in all this? And does it help if there is, or make any difference?

The lack of any purpose in suffering of any sort is a real difficulty. In fact, to a great extent, the lack of purpose *is* the suffering. I remember reading about several young servicewomen, Israeli I think, who were captured by a terrorist organization and imprisoned for a period of weeks. Eventually they were rescued, or released under some agreement, and it became known that during their internment they had been raped. Following their release, they were examined and treated for the trauma they had undergone, but it was noted that they appeared to be suffering far less emotional damage than would have been expected. These women felt that what had happened was a cost of war and so they had been able to face even rape as soldiers, rather than passive victims. Initially anyway, they were able to cope with the abuse far more easily because of this. To suffer for a cause, or for the sake of another person, is one thing; suffering to no purpose is very hard. Those who have written about the holocaust encourage me to believe that even when there cannot be any suggestion of a grand design, it is possible to find our own meaning. That *that* is the work we are called to in our situation.

Of course, when the shock is new or the pain or grief at crisis point, there is no help in suggesting that there is an exciting voyage of discovery to make. But for me, the possibility that there is some truth here, something to find, is a challenge

X If suffering is part of a GRAND DESIGN then what is the point of praying to God for relief of suffering?

I want to explore. Although, of course, I still react to others making the suggestion or commenting that God wants to reveal something or do me some spiritual good. It is different when we reach that point ourselves, and are ready to look at what might be gained in a situation. Not that there is a common purpose for all, or one right answer. It may be that the best we can do is to hope that there may be something to be found some day. Rabbi Kushner reached the conclusion that we need to discover a new way of asking our questions:

> The word 'answer' can mean 'response' as well as 'explanation', and in that sense, there may well be a satisfying answer to the tragedies in our lives. The response would be ... to forgive the world for not being perfect, to forgive God for not making a better world, to reach out to the people around us, and to go on living despite it all.[7]

In the end the choice is ours. We are free to wrest some purpose from our situation or give up on it. Like Jacob, returning home after all his trickery and finding himself alone at nightfall, we can wrestle with God, holding on until daybreak and insisting: 'I will not let you go, unless you bless me.'[8] The alternative is to turn away into cynicism and depression. As a teenager, wallowing in angst, I toyed with the possibility that life might be meaningless. Later there were still moments when faith seemed a delusion and these were intensified by cancer. My lingering sense of unworthiness and fragile self-confidence meant that knocks of any kind could tip me into depression, and fears and questions intensified the black moods: *Last week I was told that Margaret was ill with cancer. It seems her prognosis is poor. I went to see her. She is a woman in her early fifties, one of the deacons, a friendly, lively person. She had had an operation on the Monday, but was very sick, restless and exhausted and I only stayed a few minutes. I told her I brought everyone's love and she talked about being sorry to miss the meeting. I couldn't understand what she meant. 'What meeting?' I thought, but just smiled* and kissed her goodbye. On the way home, it struck me – she was talking about a women deacons' meeting planned for next May, months away. She was dying and she knew it, she was saying goodbye. I was appalled. I drove through the country lanes, lined with red and gold and buff-bright trees. The afternoon sky was dark, with shafts of pale sun and the black boughs were wild and tossing. The greens ranged from softest olive to strong flashing steam-engine-bold. It was all so beautiful. 'Death is an obscenity amongst all this,' I wept as I drove home. 'No god can have made all this and let death reign, it is a disgrace, a foul and filthy excrement.' I raved and sobbed – for me of course, as well as for Margaret. She died next morning.

I go on and on and find no real or lasting answer: 'What is life about in the face of death?' I had it all so pat until the threat of death touched me. Timor mortis conturbat me – the fear of death disturbs me. Rather more than disturbs; that's too weak a word. Death leers and peeks, mocks and sneers. I have one little hope; I cannot 'not believe' in Christ's resurrection. That is all the faith that I know, that I am sure about. But so many disbelieve, that it feels a slim and insignificant hope. I feel alone. Holy Spirit comfort me. — *I agree with this*

I do not think I was uniquely negative or self destructive. The fear of existing only to die, of being an insignificant speck in a purposeless soup of matter, lurks beneath the surface for many of us. But I have come to see that there is a choice for us, a journey offered to any who will take it. We can actively choose to believe in life, in the future, in meaning, resurrection and joy; or drift, with the constant risk of slipping into self-pity at every set-back. My illness has forced me to choose as nothing else in my life has done.

After cancer entered my life, it took me a long time to work out that my feelings of hopelessness were natural and that I do not have to take too much notice of them, they are just feelings and will pass. I am not immune to anger or terror today, and do not expect to be, but they no longer threaten me so fiercely or so constantly as they once did. I can at least *see* the choice

Death is part of life. I find no comfort in "eternal life". Jesus's death & resurrection. It wont help me cope with death!

between light and darkness, life and death, even if I cannot always make it. I do not want to be a Pollyanna, skipping through the daisies scattering gladness, but I attempt to hold to an underlying expectation that God means good towards me and towards the whole of creation.

Some time before I became ill, I organized a Saturday work-shop for undergraduates, where I was the chaplain. Two colleagues helped lead about thirty young men and women in a day of creative writing, painting, drama and liturgical dance. At the end of the day, we sat on the ground in a circle, while one person cradled a candle in the centre. We were invited to ask God the questions on our hearts, while the candle-bearer received them, but made no attempt to answer. Hesitantly at first, the questions began: 'Why do you allow wars?' 'How can you let children suffer and starve?' 'Why is my father ill?' 'What do you want for my life?' 'Do you really exist, at all?' After some minutes, I was invited to take the place of the candle-bearer in the centre of the circle. The experience was overwhelming. The questions continued, died down, then began again: 'I am lonely, where are you?' 'Why don't you show yourself?' 'What do you mean by this mess?' Hearing the anguish and reality of what was being asked, I felt an immense sorrow and love for the questioners. I had no answer, and was bidden anyway to keep silent; but I longed to say: 'I love you. I love you so much. You break my heart and I love you.' The response did not come from any sense that I *should* feel this, or an attempt to imagine what God might feel. I had not anticipated what the experience might do. It was a purely instinctive response of love, and one that any of us would make. It felt like the voice of God in me.

We seem to be implanted with a longing for the good and true and for love. Deep inside us is a reflection of the goodness of God, however hidden and twisted it may have become. Christians see the resurrection transforming Jesus' death from tragic waste to triumph, but it does not negate or undo death and suffering. The resurrection of Christ offers both a revelation and a promise: humanity *is* being made whole and suffering plays a part in this re-making, the world *will* be redeemed. Christ's agony and death reveal a purpose which does not wipe out the pains of the world, but encompasses them. Hans Küng writes of the choice that faces us if we believe in Christ:

> In the light of the suffering and death of this One who sense-lessly suffers and dies only one thing can be said, but this is decisive: even manifestly senseless suffering and death *can* have a meaning, can *acquire* a meaning. A hidden meaning. Man cannot himself attach this meaning to suffering, but he can accept it in the light of the perfect suffering and dying of this One. A meaning is not given automatically: no wishful thinking is to be satisfied, no glorification of suffering proclaimed, no tranquillisers provided and no cheap conso-lation offered. But a meaning is *offered* which can be freely accepted. Man has to decide. He can reject this – hidden – meaning: in spite, cynicism or despair. He can also accept it: in believing trust in him who endowed the senseless suffer-ing and death of Jesus with meaning. Protest, rebellion or frustration then become superfluous. Despair is at an end.[9]

This has always been God's message. 'Therefore choose life!'[10] urge the Hebrew scriptures, for God is good and has created us for good. He is committed to us and will not desert us or leave us alone. Julian of Norwich lived and wrote in fourteenth-century England when most sickness was incur-able and political stability unknown, life was frequently short and brutal. During a serious illness, when Julian was thought to be dying, she received sixteen 'shewings' or visions from God, many of which focussed on Christ's dying agony on the cross. For the rest of her life, Julian lived as an anchoress, walled up in her cell in Norwich. She devoted herself to prayer and to giving spiritual advice to those who sought her out, continuing to meditate on her visions for sixteen years before writing the *Revelations of Divine Love*, the first extant book to be written in English by a woman:

Would you know your Lord's meaning in this? Learn it well. Love was his meaning. Who showed it you? Love. What did he show you? Love. Why did he show you? For love. Hold fast to this, and you shall learn and know more about love, but you will never need to know or understand about anything else for ever and ever. Thus did I learn that love was our Lord's meaning.[11]

I believe this, too

Suffering is one of the
(+ proof!)
Consequences, of God's
non-intervention in
the laws of nature

7

Carrying the Cross

The worst time was when the cancer first came back. I had been afraid all along that it would, afraid I was not doing it right, afraid of my fear, afraid of death. But time went on and the gap between check-ups lengthened. It was nearly four years before I found the new tiny lump, this time in my armpit. It seemed more than I could cope with. Was this my fault then? Had I unconsciously willed the cancer to return? If only I had eaten differently, exercised more, kept a permanently positive outlook, forgiven my siblings or parents or friends, learnt relaxation techniques, worked on expressing my feelings, accepted myself, had greater faith – in short been a different person, then perhaps this terror would not have returned. But it did. Following minor surgery, I was advised that treating my ovaries with radiotherapy would be a good safeguard against further invasion of the disease, cutting down the production of female hormones on which many breast cancers thrive. I was in my early forties and had no desire to enlarge our family, but my sense of femininity felt doubly attacked. I had already had surgery to my breast. Now, in a few days of treatment, I was to be precipitated into the menopause. I wrote: *Two weeks ago I went back to the hospital and had radiotherapy on my ovaries. I nearly finished that sentence: to stop me being a woman. I suppose that is what I feel has happened. I hated it, lying on the metal bench, listening to the machine humming and knowing it was killing a perfectly healthy, life-giving, right-functioning part of me. It made me very angry. It also made me feel very sick, much worse than I expected or remembered from last time I had radiotherapy.*

Afterwards I was desolate. Somehow I felt that I had been weighed and found wanting as a woman, a Christian and a human being. I had always been sensitive about my female identity. A lanky, late developer, I had worried endlessly in my teens that I was not normal and feared that I might never start my periods or develop a figure. Even when puberty finally arrived, I was dissatisfied with myself and unsure that anyone would desire me. Through my early and mid teens I hid behind large jumpers and a sarcastic tongue and longed for romance. Although I had done some work on these feelings in the intervening years, cancer felt like a horrible judgment: 'You didn't appreciate what you had, so you don't deserve a matching pair of breasts. You rejected your womanhood for years, now do without it!' The recurrence of cancer seemed to expose me as a fake and a failure at every level.

On the surface I continued as usual, making light of the treatment and hiding my distress and confusion. I wrote: *The first time I was ill, I tried to put it all behind me as soon as I was up and about. I didn't feel that I could do this very well and was ashamed of making a fuss, though I don't know who saw my distress except George and one or two others. Gradually the experience did recede and cancer stopped being the one defining fact about me. Now I want to treat this recurrence in the same way, but I know I cannot. The only way to be positive is to take the problem seriously (you mean I wasn't?). I mean that now I have to take cancer into account. It's not 'I had cancer, I hope it won't come back.' It's 'I have cancer, I have to find out about it, live with it, actively fight it.' Whatever that means. All that stuff about visualizing tumours being attacked by little blue soldiers seems totally naff to me. And who wants to become a 'cancer-person'? I don't want to go around rattling tins and campaigning. I just want my ordinary life back. Illness disgusts and bores me.*

About six months after the radiotherapy I went on retreat. It was the longest I had yet attempted, eight days of silence. I had taken a pile of books and letters to answer, but was advised not to read or to do anything that would occupy my thoughts or distract me; just to give space for God. Each day I met with a nun who suggested Bible passages I might ponder, listened and encouraged me; she helped me to be aware of what God might be trying to say to me. Apart from a short service every morning my time was my own, to walk, sleep, sit quiet, paint or work with clay, or just *be*. On the Friday, towards the end of the eight days, the Sister suggested spending the day thinking about the passion and death of Christ and that I might benefit from choosing to 'accompany him in his agony'. I really did not want to. I had spent the first part of the week moving away from thoughts of illness and death; discovering the present gift of God in the squirrels chasing in the grass, a peacock crying from a shed roof and a heron perched on the island in the pond. Ducks, beech trees, ponies and newly discovered ice-cream Bounty bars had delighted my afternoon walks and spoken to me of God's love. I was sorry to be asked to return to dwelling on pain and misery. However, so far things had gone well, so I thought that I had better try to do as I had been directed: *I began reading through the passages on Gethsemane. 'Go and share it with him,' the Sister had said. But it was my cry of – I can't bear it, that I heard. My plea – I don't want this, take away my sense of being hunted and marked down, I don't want to go on dealing with this; take the cancer away, I don't want to die; take the cup away! I felt depressed, unwilling to be plunged into such morbid thoughts and could not see how summoning up my own pain could be described as 'accompanying Jesus'. It was my own only too familiar agony that I was entering. Walking that afternoon, I discovered a stile and footpath across a field of young barley. The farmer had planted right up to the path, leaving a straight narrow route between the green, waist-high shoots which flanked either side. I crossed the field, remembering again that I was to meditate on the events of Good Friday. Looking ahead at this narrow pathway, I was reminded of Simon of Cyrene, pressed into carrying Christ's cross along the road to Golgotha.[1] Immediately and without any conscious connection, I was back in the Radiotherapy*

Unit. I did not want this machine killing my ovaries, burning and withering them, putting to death what was life in me. I was angry and resentful, I felt I did not want to carry this horror and death. Unexpectedly I found myself offering the memory, the unwillingness, the pain of all that the experience had meant to me. I don't know what use it can be or what I mean by this, but I offer it. It is my cross, my desolation and shame, my death instrument – not yours, but I offer it.

In the barley field my grieving and outrage for the early loss of my fertility and stolen womanhood somehow became linked with the burden of Christ's cross. Quite unexpectedly I found myself sharing in Christ's passion, that it had been given to me to carry the cross in place of Simon. I felt as if my little loss was joined to the suffering of Jesus and that I was being given the opportunity to shoulder the load for and with him. It might sound bizarre, odd, wrong, unorthodox, unbelievable, but that was what had happened, unlooked for and unexpected. I had become used to the idea that Jesus shared in our sorrows. I had never heard anyone suggest that I might share in *his*. Or rather, I thought that I had not. Searching the scriptures and looking into the writings of the mystics, I found that the idea was not new.

For years I had loved the verses from Philippians:

Yet whatever gains I had, these I have come to regard as loss because of Christ . . . For his sake I have suffered the loss of all things, and I regard them as rubbish, in order that I may gain Christ and be found in him, not having a righteousness of my own that comes from the law, but one that comes through faith in Christ, the righteousness from God based on faith. I want to know Christ and the power of his resurrection . . . [2]

Now, as if for the first time, I noticed the second half of verse 10: 'I want to know Christ and the power of his resurrection *and the sharing of his sufferings by becoming like him in his death.*' Of course, Paul, writing from prison, had a strong sense of his sufferings being *for* Christ. The trials he so graphically lists in Corinthians: 'afflictions, hardships, calamities, beatings, imprisonments, riots, labours, sleepless nights, hunger',[3] come to him as a Christian in a hostile world, challenging the customs and convictions of his day. Paul's only reference to an illness is when he calls it 'a messenger of Satan'.[4] But the concept of suffering for and even *with* Christ is there in the epistles and repeated several times. In Colossians the idea is developed further: 'I am now rejoicing in my sufferings for your sake, and in my flesh I am completing what is lacking in Christ's afflictions for the sake of his body, that is, the church.'[5] The idea of weakness as a badge of our status as Christ's servants runs through the New Testament: but it comes in a minor key that is often glossed over or ignored.[6]

I had come to accept that Christians are not to expect preferential treatment or an easy time. Now I began to see that one way of understanding pain or distress is to see our difficulties as sharing with Christ in his own passion. A clue to this identification between Christ and his followers comes in all three of the accounts of Paul's conversion in Acts. Each one describes his vision of the resurrected Lord Jesus confronting him with the words 'Why do you persecute *me?*'[7] Yet clearly the persecution had been of Jesus' followers not of Christ. Paul only came into the picture after the resurrection. The New Testament seems to blur the distinction between Christ and the Christian in a way that we struggle to grasp. Perhaps we dare not.

Despite these pointers in the Bible, it took me some time to understand what I had begun to glimpse on my retreat. I was nervous of thinking that human beings might be allowed to bear Christ's cross *with* him? Could our pains really be offered as a part of his cross? Surely this was blasphemy, masochism or a Messiah complex. But the idea remained with me. Later that year I wrote: *Never forget how it feels to be powerless. We do, of course, as quick as we can. But now, I offer the experience as all I have to offer. Not to pay off my sins, I don't*

*mean that at all. My sins are not at stake here, not the point;
God has to judge or forgive them as he will, there's nothing I
can do about them! This is separate, an experience of suffering, however insignificant when weighed on the scales of the
world's sorrow, and I am to offer it. I don't understand what
the point is, or what 'offering it' means or does, but I offer it.
Am I dumping it, trying to lose it? It doesn't seem that way,
but more of an act of participation, an attempt to share
Christ's, or the world's pain. There is such good, beauty, love
and joy in the world – as well as agony and hunger and death.
Somehow to offer to share in the darkness, rather than to react
against it, seems like an affirmation of the light. As if I am
saying that love IS stronger than hate, life than death, On my
retreat, the radiotherapy had suddenly felt the same as Simon
carrying Christ's cross. It was a parallel for me of having to
take on death when I didn't want to; the death of my healthy
ovaries, of my fertility, or womanhood, a death imposed.
Now I look back and see other connections that I have made
with Christ's pain. I remember George's words, when I was
first in hospital and wept about the operation on my breast.
He talked of Jesus' disfigurement and I was comforted
without knowing why. If a doctor is brusque or dismissive a
check-up can sometimes seem like being mocked; it did today.*

Of course there are dangers here. We are rightly suspicious
of the sort of piety that encourages a masochistic pleasure in
pain, or a passive acceptance. The image of languishing
Victorian ladies making much of their 'cross' does not represent a healthy approach to life, and all sorts of illness or
difficulty can be used by individuals to manipulate and control
others. I am well aware of that. On the other hand, the
powerful can be manipulative as well. The poor were once
encouraged to look to heaven for their reward; and the church
taught that injustice and deprivation must be silently and
patiently borne. So it seems that the charge of manipulation
can be levelled at oppressors at least as often as at the
oppressed. But I am talking about something different from
either masochism or oppression; not a wish to suffer, but a

belief that, if suffering is unavoidable, it can be offered to God. A hope that, freely offered in this way, our pains can be used in the divine economy and order.

In the previous chapter, I quoted Victor Frankl's view that as well as our work and our relationships, suffering can give meaning to our lives. However he is adamant that suffering is to be resisted if at all possible:

> But let me make it perfectly clear that in no way is suffering necessary to find meaning. I only insist that meaning is possible even in spite of suffering – provided, certainly, that the suffering is unavoidable. If it were avoidable, however, the meaningful thing to do would be to remove its cause, be it psychological, biological or political. To suffer unnecessarily is masochistic rather than heroic.[8]

Frankl is right. There is nothing good about suffering in itself and the healthy response is to avoid it if at all possible. While we need to face the reality of our sorrows, we may also need the chance to get away from them and too much sympathy can be as hard to handle as too little. A friend talked of his wife's death and how swamped he felt by others' kindness: 'The best thing for me was when a mate brought round a bottle of whisky, said he was sorry and changed the subject.'

Society is quick to label people *victims*, in a way that separates those who are suffering or disadvantaged. Whilst identifying with a group can be a useful support or gain attention for taking action, victim terminology has its pitfalls. I am uneasy being labelled a *cancer victim*, as if that is all that I am, or that I have to be a victim all the time. It is all too easy to focus on our own difficulties when things are bad and submerge our whole identity in the problem. The media often underlines this unhealthy focus. 'So-and-so has lost or won his/her battle with alcohol, cancer or multiple sclerosis,' blare the headlines, and 'X was an *innocent* victim of Aids, or child abuse.' The stereotypes of fighting, triumph or defeat may or may not be appropriate; and the term *innocent* begs the question for me. Who is innocent? What is guilty? Are some afflictions, then, the just punishment for misdoings? I think not.

A few years ago there was much coverage of the case of a child, known only as Jamie B., who had a rare form of leukaemia and needed a particular drug which the Health Service refused to provide. Apparently the drug could only painfully prolong her life for a few months. Her father took her case to court, and the papers were full of accolades for 'Brave Jamie', 'This little girl's amazing courage!' and 'What a fighter!' Interviewed on television, the ten-year-old remarked that she was not brave at all: 'You'd all the be the same,' she said. 'It's not that I'm brave, I just want to live, that's all.' She expressed it very well. Suffering does not automatically make anyone a hero, any more than it makes them a victim.

We appear to take a universally positive, if somewhat sugary, attitude to those who suffer, at least on the surface. Perhaps, by labelling individuals as victims, we are attempting to distance ourselves from them and from our own fears. I have certainly felt this when individuals are quick to offer solutions, as if reassuring themselves that they will not be touched in the same way. The situation for survivors of the holocaust arriving in the new Israel highlights some of the hidden attitudes which we may need to face:

The new immigrants had some surprises for me . . . 'They don't like us, won't accept us,' some told me. Astonished, I asked them to elaborate, and when they did, it hurt . . . They were made to feel that they themselves were to blame for their suffering: They should have left Europe earlier, as they had been advised to do, or risen up against the Germans. In other words, the immigrants were seen to embody what young Jews in Palestine refused to be: victims. As such they represented the saddest image in Jewish history: the weak, stooped Jew in need of protection. They personified the Diaspora and its indignities.

'We came here hoping to escape humiliation,' a former

teacher from Lodz told me. 'But in their eyes I am human wreckage,' a former merchant from Radom told me sadly.[9]

So the human impulse to avoid pain and weakness is two-edged. To glorify suffering, our own or that of others, is unhealthy and perverse; but to avoid those who suffer because they make us uncomfortable is a cruel rejection. Instead we have to be prepared to take on the suffering of others in some way. Faced with tragedy, as Frankl asserts, we are to develop a 'tragic optimism':

> An optimism in the face of tragedy and in view of the human potential which at its best always allows for: 1) turning suffering into a human achievement and accomplishment; 2) deriving from guilt the opportunity to change oneself for the better; 3) deriving from life's transitoriness an incentive to take responsible action.[10]

We are quick to recognize and salute those who come into the first of Frankl's categories, overcoming difficulties or physical impairment and using their situation for the good of all. We occasionally witness the second, in the rehabilitation of public figures who have endured disgrace and made restitution by dedicated service. The third alternative, 'deriving from life's transitoriness an incentive to take responsible action', is perhaps a little harder to grasp:

> The third aspect of the tragic triad concerns death. But it concerns life as well, for at any time each of the moments of which life consists is dying, and that moment will never recur. And yet is not this transitoriness a reminder that challenges us to make the best possible use of each moment of our lives? . . . To be sure, people tend to see only the stubble fields of transitoriness but overlook and forget the full granaries of the past into which they have brought the harvest of their lives: the deeds done, the loves loved, and last but not least, the sufferings they have gone through with courage and dignity.[11]

Frankl here sees the fact of death as a spur to value life, to savour each moment. A few weeks before his death, the dramatist Dennis Potter gave a television interview. He knew he was soon to die and spoke of his drive to complete his final play, but also of the tree below the window where he worked that spring and of 'the blossomiest blossom ever'. Potter's ability to communicate the significance and beauty of life, in the face of death, was immensely moving. The fact that he was dying gave every word power and meaning.

The way in which individuals face suffering can inspire and encourage us and may give them a sense of purpose. Our fear is that we might not possess such stoic courage. How will I respond when no action is possible; when there are no longer any decisions to take, but only an on-going endurance? Perhaps this question has continued to haunt me because I am not yet 'there' and imminent death appears to be still some way off! But I am forced to grapple with the problem. When suffering is unavoidable, what are we to do with our fear and pain? Will death, or a situation of total helplessness, take all meaning from life? Is it possible, then, to find a purpose through sharing in the agony of Christ?

On occasions I have worked with groups of people looking at the question of suffering and been surprised at their resistance to the idea that their experience is significant. Sometimes I have invited them to consider the events of Jesus' passion and how they might have shared in it and they are quick to respond with suggestions that they would have betrayed Christ, abandoned him or denied him. No doubt this is true, so might I. They find it very much harder to acknowledge that they may have suffered with him. I want to suggest that all of us know some experience of suffering and so have shared with Christ. We may have gone through intense and hopeless loneliness, as Jesus did in the garden while his friends slept, been betrayed by those we counted as close, or felt imprisoned by circumstances or expectations. We too may have faced unjust criticism and accusations, whether as children when no one else owned up, or as adults; we may have known the icy cold

of exposure and felt the weight of burdens too heavy to bear;
we may have been ground down by systems, and seen organizations or bureaucracy crushing our cherished hopes. I am
not suggesting that any or all of these have been shattering
experiences, though some may have been, or that every person
will identify with every scenario. Only that these are not
unfamiliar to us, not strange; that as well as being spurred to
change the situation and to work against oppression, perhaps
we are also offered the possibility of being *with* Christ in these
events. Our sorrows, failure and weakness can be given into
God's hands as a conscious sharing with his pain, made real
and concrete at the cross. I believe that we are offered the
privilege, if we will, of sharing with Christ in his agony; of
bearing with him the weight of a wounded world.

Mary Craig describes something of this in her own exploration of suffering:

> In the standing still, in the acceptance of the unavoidable
> moment in all its bleakness, lies the possibility of salvation
> and growth for ourselves and for others. We can say to
> whatever deity we pray to, 'For what it's worth, here it is.
> Take it and use it. Use it for the hungry, the homeless, the
> lonely; for the man down the road who has lost both his job
> and his wife; for the friend whose little girl has been killed.
> Use it to help me understand, to be less self centred, more
> loving.'
>
> Heaven knows, we may be feeling so wretched that we
> have to do violence to ourselves to utter such a prayer. We
> may do so through clenched teeth. But if we ever hope one
> day to mean what we say, we are expressing a trust that one
> day, though not yet, all will be well; and all will finally be
> well. On that day we shall at last 'arrive where we started'
> and know what it is to be whole.[12]

Since that connection was first made for me in the field of
green barley, I have glimpsed it again at other times of real
distress. When, told the following year, that further cells had

been found and more treatment was needed, I experienced a sense of being trapped in a tightening net. My immediate reaction was to identify with the terror of being taken, hemmed in by the impersonal uniforms of soldiers; nowhere to run, an inexorable fate coming to take me. Again, following major back surgery, I seemed to lie in the tomb with the dead Christ, powerless to make a move, and utterly dependent on others in every way.

As I have come to think about unavoidable suffering as a way of sharing in the passion of Christ, I have become freshly aware of the theme in Christian teaching and spirituality. It runs through the pages of scripture[13] and the writings of teachers and mystics through the ages. It is not new. 'The cup that I drink you will drink; and with the baptism with which I am baptized, you will be baptized,' promised Jesus;[14] and to Peter: 'You used to fasten your own belt and go wherever you wished. But when you grow old, you will stretch out your hands, and someone else will fasten a belt around you and take you where you do not wish to go.'[15]

Jürgen Moltmann, in his exploration of the significance of the cross of Christ, reminds us of the tradition of the suffering in mysticism, that came to full flowering in the Middle Ages:

> Thus by meditation and adoration people have drawn closer to the sufferings of Christ, participated in them and felt them as their own sufferings . . . This spiritual absorption into the suffering of Christ led, as late mediaeval mysticism said, to a conformity of the soul with the crucified Christ . . . In the later Middle Ages, the Christian people of Europe were seized by this devotion to the passion . . . The 'man of sorrows' spoke to those who were wasting away in pain, and to whom no one else spoke, because no one could help them. In representations of the crucified Christ, the emphasis moved from sacramental devotion to his victory on the cross to inward devotion to his sacrificial death on the cross. These images of the crucifixion, such as that upon the Isenheim altar, were not merely the artistic

expression of a new form of devotion, but at that time were regarded as miracle working images. The sick, the cripples and the incurables were brought before these images, and in their worship there they experienced relief from their sufferings and healings . . . This mysticism of the passion has discovered a truth about Christ which ought not to be suppressed by being understood in a superficial way. It can be summed up by saying that suffering is overcome by suffering, and wounds are healed by wounds. For the suffering in suffering is the lack of love, and the wounds in wounds are the abandonment. And the powerlessness in pain is unbelief.[16]

In our day, we are wary of the idea of sharing in Christ's passion, fearing it as an excuse for masochistic revelling or oppression of others. Instead we prefer to emphasize the positive, the joy of new life in Christ and the resurrection victory. We hope that this offers a more attractive picture of the Christian faith, attempting to combat the prevailing image of the church as an outdated killjoy institution, which is preoccupied with guilt and internal squabbles. And yet, I wonder if the constant demand for the church to 'make a stand' and 'give a strong lead', when clearly the last thing that people really want is to be told how to live their lives, is actually a longing for the church to speak about reality and the pain of life. There is a sense that our popular culture already offers a torrent of words on living life to the full and having a positive outlook. Perhaps what is wanted is some engagement with the dark side of human experience. We may try to ignore it, but the fact of death and suffering is there for all of us. The one place where people might hope to have evil, pain, frailty and death taken seriously is the church. The cross has been out of fashion, it may be time to redress the balance. It is time in my life. — *If you are seriously in or dying - may be! But not otherwise*

As we have already seen, the nights of the spirit form a large part of our sharing in the cross. In the active night the cross will never be far away if our joy in God is to contain and take precedence over other joys. We carry it through life as gently and steadily as we can, picking it up again whenever we let it fall through sin, negligence or weakness. Here we are, to a certain extent in control . . . In the passive night of the spirit, however, we find ourselves nailed to the cross which we probably have not chosen. Our only choice lies in whether we bear it in the spirit of the repentant or the un-repentant thieves who were both crucified with Jesus.

Whatever cross we are crucified on, whether it be one of our own or someone else's making, does not ultimately matter. What does matter is that we do not try to bear it alone, for it is part of Christ's cross and that of suffering creation. His life is ours and our pain is his when borne in solidarity with everyone else's. It is there that we find joy at the heart of darkness.[17]

Perhaps, if I were _dying_
but of course there can
be no joy in suffering!

Why do men have to
suffer? (See Leslie Weatherhead)

8

Acceptance

[handwritten margin note, left: We are subject to the laws of Nature]

[handwritten margin note, right: of which the laws of nature a part — + God does not interfere with them!]

We are puny, dependent beings, a part of the created order that lives, flourishes and dies. The real puzzle is not so much why this should be, but why this seems to be so hard for us to accept. We have always known our situation and yet it causes us grief and heartache. Human beings seem to be born with a desire for *more*, burdened with a divine discontent, at once the cause of our triumphs over the limitations of nature and our greatest sorrow. An autumn walk can wonderfully restore my sense of proportion. There lies the pattern before me: the turning leaves; the fruit swelling from the swiftly shed blossom; the rotting down of dead wood and bark and plant life into rich earth and the knowledge of the coming spring. And within the pattern there is an infinite variety, so that no two leaves are the same shape or size, receive precisely the same amount of sunlight or fall at the same moment. Kicking the leaves and marvelling at the colours, I am content to see my life as part of the created order, unique and precious but limited by an apparently arbitrary mortality. But autumnal musings are very little help; when faced with threat to child or loved one; fear of the future; or failure, shame, bodily weakness or death.

Throughout this book I have tried to draw a parallel between my own experience of illness and that of bereavement. I have gone through shock and anger, the heaviness of depression and endless searching for answers. All these now seem to have been necessary stages on a journey, but as I have moved on from my first horror and unbelief to an acceptance of sorts, the question remains: what kind of acceptance is healthy? Is it possible to distinguish between a positive life-affirming acceptance and simply becoming resigned?

Within my own surroundings, living at my own pace, I hardly notice my limitations. Only when I try to keep up with those who are fit, do I become aware that I have to have extra rest and become frustrated. Recently, George and I led a pilgrimage tour to the Middle East. It was wonderful to be in Damascus and walk the 'Street called Straight', to cross the Syrian desert and wander through green glades high up among the cedars of Lebanon. Although the days were tiring, I am used to going to bed at the earliest possible moment and was content to spend our free day resting, rather than making a precarious excursion on the Euphrates in what looked like a wash tub! The problem came one evening when we were staying by the Mediterranean. We had had a full day touring and exploring but returned with an hour or two to spare before dinner. The hotel overlooked the sea, it was beautifully warm and the salt-water hotel pool below the balcony was peopled with friends from our party, splashing and relaxing together. I longed to join them, I liked them, they were having fun and it looked so perfect in the water; but I knew I was already exhausted. I found no peaceful acceptance that afternoon; instead I was furious, resentful, bitter, childishly tearful and thoroughly ashamed of myself. So my halting journey towards peace is still slow and confused, with numerous detours to confront fears, groundless or otherwise, to protest or search for answers. But the goal has been clear from the beginning: to come to some sort of acceptance of myself and my life.

The line *is* a fine one between living with a given situation as positively and hopefully as possible and lapsing into resignation. That sort of fatalism is akin to despair and can be a real temptation when we feel demoralized and exhausted. As my journal shows, I have frequently indulged in self-pity and despair and still do from time to time, but I am clear that this is very different from true acceptance. I hope that I am not deluding myself by affirming that there is an acceptance of ourselves and our situation, that says 'Yes' to life, while seeing that all things are held within the suffering love of God. We do not have to call pain and evil, good; we may not understand, but we try to trust that God can hold it all, and us in it.

The saints and mystics call this struggle to accept, or come to terms, *detachment*. They speak of the ability to take a longer view and to see ourselves held in relation to God, whatever our circumstances. Their writings offer glimpses of the spiritual pilgrimage through which we can hope to grow towards this balance. Of course, Teresa of Avila, Brother Lawrence and the rest lived in very different cultures from our own and consequently we can find their teaching difficult or remote. I need to take them in very small bites, in order to avoid becoming hopelessly depressed by the apparently unbridgeable gap between their spiritual experience and my own! But some of this is because of the disparate contexts of our lives and ways of looking at the world, as well as the obvious relative difference between our spiritual maturity. Often what they have to say is totally beyond me. Then I have to give up, at least temporarily, and not worry that I do not understand. It has helped me to realize that these folk are giants of prayer. It is as silly for me to be discouraged at the heights they have attained, as it would be to despair because I am not Mozart. We only follow after, grateful when what they have to say strikes through like a shaft of light.

Bernard of Clairvaux, one of the great teachers of the church in the twelfth century, describes our pilgrimage towards God as four stages, or degrees of love:

What are the four degrees of love? First, we love ourselves for our own sake; since we are unspiritual and of the flesh we cannot have an interest in anything that does not relate to ourselves. When we begin to see that we cannot subsist by ourselves, we begin to seek God for our own sakes. This is the second degree of love; we love God, but only for our own interests. But if we begin to worship and come to God again and again by meditating, by reading, by prayer, and by obedience, little by little God becomes known to us through experience. We enter into sweet familiarity with God, and by tasting how sweet the Lord is we pass into the third degree of love, so that now we love God, not for our own sake, but for himself. It should be noted that in this third degree we will stand still for a very long time.

I am not certain that the fourth degree of love in which we love ourselves for the sake of God may be perfectly attained in this life. But, when it does happen, we will experience the joy of the Lord and be forgetful of ourselves in a wonderful way. We are, for those moments, one mind and one spirit with God.[1]

I would like to think that I love God for God's own sake, but know that mostly I love him for my own. There are only tiny, brief moments when I lose awareness of myself and can give myself to God unreservedly. But if we can reach that third degree of love, we shall be content whatever is happening around us. It is a goal to look towards; to love God for himself alone, seeing him in all things, looking to him in all situations, and finally learning to love even ourselves as part of God's beloved creation. However, even Bernard did not expect to reach the fourth degree and find complete freedom from self-obsession and self-preoccupation and we may be forgiven for lagging a little behind. If you are like me, you will need plenty of encouragement along the way. In 1980 my spiritual director was writing to me:

Losing your life in all this means more than self-denial and committal of life to him. It means handing yourself over to him so that he can recreate you . . . It's growing to be *unaware* of oneself. Only God can perform this miracle, so the quicker we let him get cracking, the better. It will take more than this life, so have patience.

But in 1990, I did not seem to have progressed very far:

Primarily, 'Losing one's life' is God's work. We co-operate. It's S-L-O-W, you will (or do!) get sick of yourself and see 'self', North, South, East and West, I do. But just keep going on. Joy comes with it as you get freer of yourself. One day you will forget yourself (be unaware of yourself) totally. What joy.

A day-by-day giving ourselves into God's hand and an unbroken trust in his goodness is the highest any of us will attain. Just occasionally we come across those who seem to manage it and who manifest a quality of serenity and childlike joy. They are often obscure people who would never dream that they are at all extraordinary, but Jesus' words seem to apply to them directly: 'Truly I tell you, unless you change and become like children, you will never enter the kingdom of heaven. Whoever becomes humble like this child is the greatest in the kingdom of heaven.'[2]

But all this talk of acceptance and trust can leave me feeling more inadequate than ever. Although I no longer search end-lessly for answers, I can still be knocked by chance remarks. 'I always think there's a reason within the *person* for their sick-ness, don't you?' commented a friend, earnestly, about some-one else who was dying of cancer. Another acquaintance advised me: 'You have to treat the underlying cause of disease, cancer means that part of your life is out of control.' Someone else recently lent me some tapes on healing. I braced myself for the inevitable reference to cancer and was not surprised to hear that 'hidden resentments are the primary cause'. Once those sort of statements would reduce me to a self-condemned wreck for days. It is a little easier now to recover my balance, but still takes energy and heart searching. I know that I am vulnerable to the judgments of others, and accept that I am prone to self-pity and become afraid if I am inexplicably unwell. I am not constantly filled with inner peace, but I have perhaps gone some way to accepting that I am human.

A few years ago I wrote: *Yesterday I phoned a woman called Sue. She has just had a mastectomy and I was asked to* contact her, presumably to make comforting and encouraging noises. 'It has been such a witness!' she exclaimed. 'Everyone is so amazed that I have such peace and joy. I am able to tell everyone that God is so loving . . .' I felt small and feeble. I didn't witness like that. I am not jealous – yes you are, you liar. Of course, I am jealous of the way people will think well of her. But, at the same time, I know I could not have been different and that my struggles have been real and the only way for me to react. I could not have rested happily in: 'God is so loving,' full stop. Although, funnily, I hope to get there. I almost do get there from time to time! In fact looking back five years to my first illness, I think I did say 'God is so loving,' now and again, in between the howls. True, it sounded a bit hollow. It was my defence against the calamity that had struck me. I need not be jealous of her serenity, or of her 'getting it right'. I am as I am, and God deals with me as I am. I know that I am feeble, failing and faithless much of the time, but in a weird way I would not have missed any of the pain of that. I am faithless, but he is faithful.

T. H. White's classic tale *The Once and Future King* contains some glorious stories of Arthur's childhood adventures when, in preparation for a wise reign, he is turned into various animals by Merlin. He becomes in turn a perch, an ant, a merlin, a wild goose and a badger; and so comes to hear the creation myth of the badgers. 'The Badger's Story' tells of how, at the very beginning, the first half-formed embryos were summoned before God and told to choose what sort of tools or defence they would like to be given:

'They were allowed two or three specializations, so that some chose to use their arms as flying machines and their mouths as weapons . . . We badgers thought very hard and decided to ask three boons. We wanted to change our skins to shields, our mouths for weapons, and our arms for garden forks . . . Just before it was time to knock off for Sunday, they had got through all the little embryos except one. This embryo was Man . . .

"Please God," said the embryo, "I think that You have made me in the shape which I now have for reasons best known to Yourselves and that it would be rude to change . . ."

"Well done," exclaimed the Creator in delighted tones. "Here, all you embryos, come here with your beaks and whatnots and look upon Our first Man. He is the only one who has guessed Our riddle . . . As for you, Man, you will be a naked tool all your life . . . Eternally undeveloped, you will always remain potential in Our image, able to see some of Our sorrows and to feel some of Our joys. We are partly sorry for you, Man, but partly hopeful. Run along then, and do your best. And listen, Man, before you go . . ."

"Well?" asked Adam, turning back from his dismissal.

"We were only going to say," said God shyly, twisting Their hands together. "Well, We were just going to say, God bless you.'"[3]

Amongst all God's creatures, we are peculiarly naked and defenceless and of course it is our weakness that has made us strong: 'You will be a naked tool all your life, though a user of tools. You will look like an embryo till they bury you, yet all the others will be embryos before your might.'[4]

It seems that this paradox repeats itself in the spiritual world. Paul famously writes: 'Whenever I am weak, then I am strong.'[5] This is sometimes quoted like a cosy Christian proverb rather than an idea to take seriously. In fact, sadly, Paul's words are often used as a denial of weakness, an affirmation that if we have enough faith, God will supply supernatural strength when we need it. Perhaps it is not surprising that so many Christians suffer from burn-out, when we misread scripture in this way. For years I believed that I should comply with any request to do something 'for God', even if I were already over-stretched. Somehow, I reasoned, I would find the necessary energy and made a habit of relying on my ability to push myself to get me through the workload. Of course, this is not uncommon and is sometimes genuinely

*So it depends upon us — not God!!

unavoidable, but I now realize how often I made a virtue of stress and confused a burst of adrenalin with the grace of the Holy Spirit. Often Paul's paradoxical words are linked to the passage from Philippians when he writes: 'I can do all things through Christ who strengthens me.'[6] We conveniently ignore the fact that Paul is writing here from prison, where he manifestly was *not* able to leap every barrier and overcome all weakness. Instead Paul is speaking about learning to accept the circumstances of his life, whether need or plenty, and presumably freedom or confinement, strength or frailty.

In the same way, the life of Jesus also offers a very different model of ministry from that of the average well-defended and over-busy Christian. Early in Mark's Gospel, when the disciples come with stories of the sick lining up for healing, Jesus responds: 'Let us go on to the neighbouring towns, so that I may proclaim the message there also.'[7] I find this a very refreshing and releasing remark; clearly Jesus is following his own, or God's, agenda and does not feel the need to respond to every demand. John's Gospel includes an account of Jesus resting by the well, while the disciples go on into the town to find some lunch, because he is: 'tired out by his journey'.[8] There is no macho posturing or insistence that he can manage. All the Gospels describe Jesus being anointed with precious ointment and, in all but Luke, this takes place in the last week of his life. In Matthew, Mark and in John, where she is named as Mary of Bethany, a woman anoints Jesus' head in a priestly gesture and in each account she is criticized by the disciples for wasting money. The implication is that Jesus too is being condemned for allowing her to behave in this dramatic and extravagant fashion. But Jesus accepts the woman's ministry, acknowledging that she has brought the ointment: 'for the day of my burial',[9] or: 'she has anointed my body beforehand for its burial.'[10] It is as if Jesus is admitting his own need and sorrow as well as affirming the woman; allowing her to sense and answer his longing for comfort and understanding. He does not insist that he is fine and can cope! When we are willing, or even forced, to have our weakness exposed, we allow others to love us and that can be a precious gift to them. Our exhaustion or inability to answer every request for help is something that can be offered, a sharing in Christ's cross, along with our suffering or fear. When we reveal our own frailty it may be that we also show the face of God.

Just as we can easily be confused about the terms, weakness, strength and acceptance, we can also be unclear about what the *passion* of Christ actually means. We forget that the root meaning of *passion* is not violent emotion or intense suffering, but 'passivity'. During the last hours of his life all the Gospel accounts show Christ as almost entirely passive. This remarkable shift is the subject of W. H. Vanstone's book, *The Stature of Waiting*. He points out that throughout the Gospels, until the very end, Jesus is portrayed as completely in control of every situation. He has chosen his disciples, preached, healed the sick, confronted and confounded his critics, calmed the storm, taught and travelled at will; making the decisions for his own life, as well as the lives of others. Suddenly, in the Garden of Gethsemane, everything changes:

> From the moment when Jesus is handed over in the garden, Mark reports no single incident through Jesus' eyes and attributes nothing that happens to His initiative and activity. Whereas previously Mark has told us of what Jesus felt among the sceptical people of Nazareth and of what He thought . . . Now he tells us nothing whatever of what Jesus thought or felt, or of how He reacted inwardly or outwardly.[11]

Mark writes of Jesus now as in every way passive rather active. Vanstone develops this theme through a study of John's account of the passion. Here the key words and ideas, present throughout the Gospel, are suddenly reversed, stressing the same reversal of the situation:

> So, according to John's account, when Jesus is handed over, the 'day' which gives freedom and opportunity to work is

succeeded by the night when there can be no more work and by the 'binding' which takes away freedom and places Jesus in the hitherto ineffective hands of others . . . Now He who has previously exercised exousia and the power to judge passes into the exousia of others and stands under their power and judgment; and now He who had previously promised and dispensed the water of life to others becomes the recipient of their refreshment . . . John is telling us what Mark tells us: that the handing over of Jesus was His transition from working to waiting upon and receiving the works of others, from the status and role of subject to that of object, from 'doing' to 'being done to'.[12]

Perhaps Paul's words about finding strength in weakness are more than a pious maxim and can really give us hope. For if God has revealed himself as working in this way, then the idea of passivity takes on a different character. If the salvation of the world is accomplished when Christ allows himself to be taken by his enemies, without any resistance, our powerlessness may be endured in a different spirit. Even our inability to cope might become less threatening and losing control need not rob us of our self-esteem. Perhaps things that we cannot dream of might be being made possible by our willingness to do nothing.

As well as *passion*, the other word related to passivity is, of course, *patience*. To have patience is considered a virtue, and listed as a fruit of the Holy Spirit's activity in us.[13] I have always seen it as rather an anaemic virtue, useful for others to exercise on my behalf, but not immediately attractive. The idea of *waiting* is a little easier for me, knowing, hoping, that there is after all some purpose in the waiting. Among the most popular Christmas cards are numerous reproductions of mediaeval and early renaissance paintings: Piero della Francesca's nativity, with blue-robed angels perched on the stable roof, or scenes of sumptuous magi and their attendants, and often a version of the annunciation. All the depictions of the nativity story, the adoration of shepherds or

Jesus showed us the power of weakness!

magi, or the flight into Egypt, can differ quite widely; but the various annunciations are surprisingly similar. Nearly always, the angel is on the left of the painting and Mary on the right and both figures are seen sideways on, facing each other. Sometimes the angel holds a flower in its hand as it bends towards Mary, but always, there is a space between them; and the space is the centre and focal point for the painting. This is very remarkable indeed. We naturally look for the main subject of a painting somewhere near the centre. We do not expect this natural focus to be a blank stretch of wall behind two figures, or occasionally a pillar between them supporting the roof. But this is what we see over and over again in the annunciation. I wonder if the space in the paintings is about the waiting? God's wait for Mary to say 'Yes'. If Christians have got it right, this moment had been in God's heart from the beginning. Everything hung upon it, from the call of Abraham through the hopes of countless prophets, preachers and holy men and women, over hundreds of years. All expectation was focussed on this moment. Heaven waited, the angels held their breath – and in the pause, with the universe dangling on her word, came the voice of a girl. Mary answered 'Yes'.

Dr Sheila Cassidy describes that 'space' for her when she was imprisoned for treating a revolutionary in Chile:

Bewildered and afraid, I faced God. I had been so sure of God's plans for me . . . it had never occurred to me that that service might be undertaken somewhere very different from where I had chosen . . .

I had written a blank cheque and invited him to do as he willed with me . . . All night I lay there and argued with myself.

You offered yourself freely. No one forced you.

Of course.

Well, then? Now your offer's been accepted.

But I didn't think it would mean this.

What did you think then? . . . perhaps he wants you just

to be here amongst the prisoners. A Christian presence.
 I hadn't thought of that . . .
 Well, what are you worried about then?
 Nothing, I suppose.
 Relax, then.
 For a while I was quiet, then it began again.
 What if they execute me?
 Well, what if they do? . . . You believe in God, don't you?
 Does it matter if you die now?
 I suppose not. But I am afraid . . . of dying.
 Why?
 I don't know.
 What is there to be afraid of?
 If you put it like that, nothing I suppose.
 Well, then,
 Could it really be that this is going to be the end of my
life?
 Of course it could.
 But I thought I'd only just begun . . . .
 I thought you had handed the reins over.
 I have. But I thought . . .
 Stop struggling, let go.[14]

Whatever is happening to me, I retain a choice. I can fight
my circumstances, and if they are bad and I have strength,
then that will be my 'Yes' to life and to God. But when there is
nothing left to do, perhaps the 'Yes' is still required, longed for
and anxiously awaited. My hope is that in our 'Yes', God
takes hold of the painful mess and turns it in his hands; to
make of it, in ways that we cannot imagine, something new.

In the passive night of spirit we cling to the hope that it is
love that has brought us to this place and love that will hold
us in it. Our place is to stay with the situation, hoping
against hope. 'In the midst of these dark and loving
afflictions, the soul feels the presence of someone and an
interior strength that so fortifies and accompanies it that

when this weight of darkness passes, it often feels alone, empty and weak' (*Night* 11.xi.7). The power of God is within the pressure, not in spite of it.[15]

It took me a long time to work out exactly what I feared so much about cancer. As I have already admitted, in the early years there were times when I used the thought of death as an escape. Later I began to be clearer: *I see that all my 'Die, die!' has not been wanting to die at all, but only to flee. To get away from conflict or depression and from myself. Reg asked me if I was afraid of the manner of death, of increasing pain and helplessness. No,' I said, blithely. 'It's not the actual dying – but the run up, over months or years.' I fear very much the long-drawn-out doom closing in, hospitals, tests, treatment, remission, more tests etc. Having said that, life is not so bad, I am well and happy and planning a trip to America, what am I whinging about?* A year later I added: *A friend wanted me to watch a video made by an actor whose wife refused chemotherapy and died at 37. One exchange struck me in particular. He made her a promise that he would stay with her and care for her at home; assuaging her fear of being sent to a hospital to die. I realized that is my fear too, of being an anonymous patient in an institution.* I was wrong all those years ago, my fear *is* of the process of dying. How will I cope if I know that I will never go outside again? If there is nothing lovely to look at, but only fading flowers and pale hospital walls? Will I go on believing *then*? If there is no breeze on my face or bright morning sunlight, and never can be any more? Those thoughts give me pause. I cannot imagine it and the idea terrifies me. Natural beauty has always lifted me and brought an automatic response of thanksgiving, a reassurance that there is a loving creator. How will I know his love, or love him in return when there is no exhilarating freedom outdoors, but only machines and stuffiness, nausea, pain, exhaustion and drowsiness?

My fear has also been to do with failure, of not *getting it right*. That may sound ridiculous; it does to me, but it is true.

So I have feared the possibility of losing my conviction that there is a God and that he is with me. I do not know why it seems so important to hang on to faith to the end. Presumably if there is a God, I can trust him to hold me if there comes a time when I can no longer hold to him. And I believe, or try to, that all that we need in terms of courage and support will be provided, when the time comes. Surely I do not really expect to be judged on the sort of figure I shall cut on my death-bed? And yet the uneasiness persists. Will I still long for God? What will love mean for me, then? Will God still *be* there for me? For if not, the leap or slide into the dark will be dark indeed.

It is the crucifixion accounts that give me courage. Scholars generally look to Mark's Gospel as the earliest and the source of much of the material in Matthew and Luke; John stands a little alone, with a separate viewpoint. Each Gospel gives enormous attention to the passion of Christ, recording events in minute detail and setting down Jesus' last words from the cross. In John's account, Christ speaks three times, commending his mother to the care of John, calling out that he is thirsty and finally giving the triumphant affirmation: 'It is finished.'[16] He has accomplished his purpose. In Luke, Jesus pronounces forgiveness for the soldiers, promises paradise to the thief and at the point of death, declares: 'Father, into your hands I commend my spirit.'[17] Again there is a sense of completion and of Jesus' acceptance of his death. But Matthew and Mark have only one painful admission, a howl of dereliction and despair. This gives me heart:

> At three o'clock Jesus cried out with a loud voice, 'Eloi, Eloi, lema sabacthani?' which means, 'My God, my God, why have you forsaken me?' . . . Then Jesus gave a loud cry and breathed his last.[18]

Sometimes it is suggested that these words mark a stage in Christ's agony, before the peaceful offering up of his life to God. It is true that they are part of the first verse of Psalm 22, which ends as an affirmation of God's faithfulness. But I take comfort from Christ's despair. If Jesus died with a question, with fear and a sense of desolation, then perhaps it will be all right if I have to. Then even a *bad* death is not beyond redemption, and need not represent a denial of all that I have believed. Perhaps to die screaming and railing at the absence of God will only be another sharing with him – who shared all things for love's sake.

My journal again: *At the Student Vocation Conference, I had to run a meditative worship with three of the students. In turn one of us was to ask each of the others: 'Who is Jesus Christ for you?' I wondered what I was going to answer, at the moment I feel as if I don't know anything about him. The dialogue began with the two students. One said: 'My best friend, I can go to always,' the other, 'A creditor, I owe him so much.' Then it came to me and I suddenly knew what I had to say: 'It's as if I was standing on a rock, and a huge wave has swept me off. I have lost my footing and I'm whirling round, no longer in control. I have to discover that Jesus is the wave as well as the rock.' That's it. And if I stop struggling he bears me up, 'lest I dash my foot . . .', but the struggle is part of it too. There is no part of my experience that Christ is not in, that he does not share. But still there are no answers. It strikes me that Jesus, too, may have struggled to get it right. Did he wonder if it HAD to be Psalm 22 and Isaiah 53? He is the pattern after all, he foreshadowed it for us. But 'it's all very well to talk', as Toad would say, or was it Mole? Someone in* The Wind in the Willows, *anyway!* At another time, I wrote: *This sentence of death is on us all, and may be carried out at any time. I may delay, defer perhaps, by good behaviour; rest, exercise and relaxation; or lessen my chances with overwork and stress. Maybe. But I am in the same position as all other beings. Only, I know it. Any day . . . ANY DAY, may come the next step to the scaffold: 'I'm sorry Mrs Baisley, there's nothing more we can do,' and the dark hole, horrid drop at the noose's end – and then? The bridge to carry me over the troubled water? The family retainer opening the door to welcome the children home? Or the lights going out, because morning is breaking at last? I don't know. I pray so.*

One other verse from the passion narratives encourages me. It comes in John's Gospel, after Christ's death. All the immediate horror was over and a kind of calm must have come to them, that exhausted quietness that falls after extremes of emotion. Each Gospel records that Jesus' body was taken away by Joseph of Arimathea, a wealthy and respectable member of the Sanhedrin. John adds that Joseph had feared aligning himself with Christ in his life time, but now, broken by the day's events, he comes with his colleague and co-sympathizer, Nicodemus, to honour this dead mad-man, hero, saint – or Messiah? Joseph begs the body from Pilate and buries Jesus in his own well-prepared tomb. The newest translations reverse the order of the words, but for once I favour the old: 'Now in the place where he was crucified, there was a garden.'[19] Sometimes all we can do is recognize that dreams have died. There has been an end and we mourn our loss, inconsolable and rocking ourselves with grief. For whatever reason, all the world that we knew and relied on has come to an end; yet, 'In the place where he was crucified, there was a garden.' In the places where we are terrified, there is a garden. At those times when life seems meaningless, there is, perhaps, a garden waiting to be dis-covered.

After the operation on my spine in 1996, I began to notice a change. For the first time in all the years, I had been *really* ill, and in need of care and nursing. As I began to recover strength I wrote: *I have come to think of all the different times I have been ill or frightened as being somehow a part of Christ's passion. This last experience was one of total helplessness. How did it fit with Christ? It felt most like being laid in the grave, a dead weight – Michelangelo's pieta. I was lifted on and off trolleys, turned in the bed, tubed and de-tubed, washed and wiped and cleaned, a body, a nothing. And, yet, in the helplessness, we are one with Christ – 'as you did it to one of the least of these . . . you did it for me.'[20] Last night Bishop Simon spoke of Victor Frankl, and the need for mean-ing; in order to redeem suffering, to enable people to bear it.*

I simply do not understand how anyone can compare their suffering with Christ's

Yes, that is all that is needed. I know now that I can endure pain and sickness, if I have to. Before, the fear of suffering haunted and crippled me, but I survived the months of agony. For the first time in my life I was really sleepless, walking up and down every night, trying to ease the pain, biting on my pillow, crying out for it to stop – and then the enemas and nausea and weakness in hospital. In that sense I am both more and less afraid. It is truly horrible and it is bearable; people are so kind, so loving. I understood for the first time the value and gift of nursing. The people who handled me with love and respect gave me dignity and restored my selfhood. I recognized their ministry and was comforted. I am amazed, still, at the love that I received. The hard thing would be to go through it and know it was not going to get better – yes that still appals me. Don't kid yourself sister, you don't have to crack it all at once! Though too, truly, the only reality is 'now'; the only contact with God, in the now. And love never fails, the only thing that lasts is the love.

As the memory of that experience of total dependence has faded, I find that my fear of the future has considerably lessened. What has remained is the knowledge that it is endurable, and that I was loved. And paradoxically, I now feel more positive about my life and health than at any time since the illness began. I do not know why this is. Perhaps I have a sense that I cannot afford to mess about with imaginary terrors; this is serious. Perhaps I am now too afraid even to feel my fear, or to face the probable future course of the disease. On the other hand, it may be that having been helpless in a hospital bed, I have discovered that it is not so scary; and out of it all, being loved is what I can best remember. Perhaps I have finally tumbled to the truth that I must live today, relishing it, sucking the joy and grit and pith out of it, being fully *in* it, while it is today. For whatever reason, I feel hopeful. Perhaps the cancer will go on being sluggish and user-friendly, or go away completely, or my immune system might wake up and chase it away. Perhaps God will cure me, heal me, after all. Years ago I wrote: *The question all this has raised is 'Am I*

why should he? why you?
why not others? He doesn't intervene
for this way

really loved?' For if I am, what am I doing here, how has this
come about? But that is the question for all of us; if we are
loved, why, how can we die? The fear of death, the fact of
death is our constant puzzle and trouble. Philosophers say
that it is death that gives meaning to life, I feel it takes mean-
ing from it. So the two thoughts hang together – What am I
doing here? What's a nice girl like me doing in a place like
this? And the steady voice: 'Daughter, Barbara, greatly
beloved, where is your faith?' We live, most of us, doing our
best and struggling to survive. We long for a future where
God's perfect will is done and the promise of light and life is
realized. It is this vision that has drawn me, made me want to
bring my life into line with God; and discover on the journey,
almost incidentally, that I am loved. Sometimes I am able to
believe it. If that remains true, then resurrection is a certainty
and we already in part inhabit it. If we are loved, then the long
wandering detour of cancer has been worth it; because it has
been my journey and because in spite of the questions and the
terror, in spite even of myself, it has been a journey towards
God.   Why does it have to be painful?

    I am reminded of Winnie Mandela on the television news,
long years before the end of apartheid and her disgrace. She
had been placed under house arrest or a banning order, I
forget which, and the camera only caught her for a moment,
before she was blocked and hustled out of the way. We had
one glimpse, just long enough to see her raise an arm and proclaim: 'We cannot *lose!*' Without consciously striving, when
we are in love with life, we become life-bringers ourselves;
those who envision, encourage and invigorate others. 'We are
God's children, now; what we will be has not yet been
revealed. What we do know is this . . . we will be like him, for
we will see him as he is.'[21] And when we are unable to do
more, when strength and light fail; then others act for us,
praying on our behalf, shouldering our loads, carrying us.
Perhaps, then, we will be closer than ever to this God who
became a dead weight on a cross and was laid in a tomb, only
to rise.

9

Today I Am Alive

Take care that you do not forget the Lord your God . . . who brought you out of the house of slavery, who led you through the great wilderness, an arid waste land with poisonous snakes and scorpions . . . to humble you and to test you, and in the end to do you good.[1]

During the years of the Second World War, C. S. Lewis became a household name through his radio broadcasts about his Christian faith, and his books became and have remained best sellers. Post-war England was an austere place, where understatement and self-control were the cherished virtues and feelings were not discussed, particularly in public. It was also a much narrower world than our own, with more rigid social divides and a distrust of the unconventional and foreign. A middle-aged Oxford academic was the last person one might have expected to fall in love with an American divorcee.

The successful film, *Shadowlands*, tells the story of C. S. Lewis' love affair and marriage to Joy Davidman, while she was dying of cancer. A BBC film, of the same name and scripted by the same author, was made some years earlier. This version of *Shadowlands* uses rather more of Lewis' own writings, focussing on his struggle to make sense of his grief at Joy's death and drawing on his book, *A Grief Observed*. A West End stage production, also written by William Nicholson, repeats the story in a different form, again examining Lewis' own faith: the journey of a Christian apologist coming face to face with his own questions, as well as his answers.

All three versions of *Shadowlands* recount the compelling
drama of the relationship between 'Jack' and Joy and in each
account Lewis is seen quoting from one of his popular talks:

funny way of showing love!

'God loves us, so he makes us the gift of suffering. Through
suffering, we release our hold on the toys of this world, and
know that our true good lies in another world.

We're like blocks of stone, out of which the sculptor
carves the forms of men. The blows of his chisel, which hurt
us so much, are what make us perfect. The suffering in the
world is not the failure of God's love for us; it is that love in
action.'[2]   *I find this incomprehensible!*

In both filmed versions Lewis quotes this passage as part of a
lecture. Nicholson uses Lewis' own words to make the point
that writing about suffering in the abstract, even as lucidly as
Lewis was able to do, is a very different matter from under-
going it. The words describing pain as the blows of God's
chisel were now coming home to roost and it was Lewis himself who was to be carved and made perfect.

In the stage play, produced at The Queens Theatre,
London, in 1989 with Nigel Hawthorne as Lewis, that excerpt
is repeated on three separate occasions. At the start of the play
Hawthorne, as Lewis, spoke from his notes with conviction
and energy, an assured speaker, confident and in control.
Later, as the play moves beyond his meeting with Joy
Davidman and the diagnosis of her cancer, he recited the same
words again. This time he faltered, his voice breaking as he
tried to retain his composure and continue with the text. On
the final occasion when we heard the passage, Joy had died.
The curtain fell leaving Hawthorne alone at the front of the
stage. Now he howled the words into the dark auditorium in
a great eruption of emotion, his raw pain exposed for all to
see. It was an unforgettable performance.

We cannot say what C. S. Lewis would have made of this
portrayal of his private life, but I imagine he would have been
horrified at the exploration of his personal feelings and his

grief. Neither can we know how accurately the author has
actually portrayed C. S. Lewis' reactions. But the dilemma
of being caught between our reasoned reflections and our
experience is one that we all know and understand. Over these
last fourteen years, I have been endeavouring to bring these
two strands together in my own life; my feelings about cancer
and some sort of objective understanding of what has been
going on for me, of what suffering might mean. As Christians,
our conviction is that God is there in the confusion. Our
hope that, for love's sake, he will remain in the muddles
and work with us to bring them, in the end, to some sort of
resolution.

Vague

'The blows of his chisel, which hurt us so much, are what
make us perfect,' quotes Nicholson's play. The biblical image
recalls Jeremiah's famous vision of God as a potter: 'The
vessel he was making of clay was spoiled in the potter's hand,
and he reworked it into another vessel, as seemed good to him.
Then the word of the Lord came to me: Can I not do with you,
O house of Israel, just as this potter has done?'[3] But the words
break down when we are the ones being chiselled or
reworked. We are indeed caught between the theory of God's
loving purpose and our pain, as Lewis himself movingly
describes in the initial shock of his bereavement:

> No, my real fear is not of materialism. If it were true,
> we . . . could get out from under the harrow. An overdose
> of sleeping pills would do it. I am more afraid that we are
> really rats in a trap. Or, worse still, rats in a laboratory . . .
> Supposing the truth were, 'God always vivisects.'[4]

As a Christian, Lewis knew God as the one who shares in
human agony, as well as perfecting us through it. The genius
of Nicholson's play is that, in watching this 'explainer' of God
on the rack himself, we witness something of God's
identification with human suffering. As the rational word-
master becomes vulnerable, his heartbreak brings his own
words to life; they become flesh in a way that they could never

*✳ I can accept this — but He does
not allow me to stop it !*

Why can't He reveal himself! Why through humans? Why through suffering?

do while remaining on the page. The play makes Lewis' words
incarnate and we see that, just as Jesus Christ declares and
makes visible the invisible God, Christians too are granted the
privilege of revealing God. That is the miracle. Our suffering
can show forth God, because in our pain we discover the inter-
change that has always existed between creator and creation,
redeemer and redeemed. God comes in Christ to live out
God's own agony and involvement in his wounded world, and
it is given to us to share in it too. 'You will know that I am
in my Father, and you in me, and I in you,'[5] says Jesus – on
the night of his arrest. These words, that we rightly use as a
picture of the deepest communion with God, the summit of
our prayer relationship, were uttered not at a cosy fireside
chat, or overlooking the tranquillity of Lake Galilee, but at the
point of Christ's entry into horror and dereliction.

Like C. S. Lewis, we know that God is in us, with us in all
things, in that sense there is nothing new, no startling discovery to be made. However, for many of us, until our
confidence is shaken to rattling point, there is always a suspi-
cion that we might have been deluding ourselves. We have
a legitimate concern that if a disaster hits, the shock and
disturbance will make what we thought was our faith look
like blind complacency. Often we are right. But the tragedy
that brings us to this moment of truth is also a call to a
journey. We are used to the idea of the journey of faith, like
Abraham, setting out 'not knowing where he was going'.[6] We
may not expect that being knocked and left sprawling by some
ghastly circumstance is also an invitation to travel. It will not
feel like it, at least initially. But there is journey for us, we can
seek to discover the meaning of what has happened to us and,
in so doing, discover something more of God.

I have not yet arrived, but I have begun. On some days I
am aware to some extent of God's presence in whatever is
happening, but mostly that is not the case. When we look back
at the worst times we see the obvious, that nothing is needed
beyond the simplest *knowing*, although we frequently come to
that simplicity through a long and difficult detour. And we do

not seem able to hold on to that glimpse for long. Mother Julian had reached the point of death and then lived out the rest of her life in solitude; there was nothing easy or comfortable about her life. It is only from this experience that she offers the simplicity of: 'I love you and you love me, and our love shall never be broken.'[7] Most of us cannot *live* by such beauty, although we may well recognize that this is the way to live. We see the possibility, but have not yet arrived. So we travel on, hopefully with our eyes a little less blinkered and with a little more confidence that the loving and sharing of God will go on being true for us in the future; that after all 'fears may be liars'.[8]

One fairy tale that has come to mean a great deal to me is the story of Sleeping Beauty and in particular the figure of the Prince, the traveller making his long arduous journey to the enchanted castle. As he battles through the sleeping forest, he has no real idea of what he will find. Perhaps there will be a beautiful sleeping maiden, as the old tales tell, or perhaps he will find only a castle of the dead. After all, it has been a hundred years since anyone has been there, nothing is known for certain. Worse, perhaps he *will* find the Princess, now an ancient crone, waiting for him like a foul spider in a web. He journeys on, undeterred by his fears, hacking and fighting his way through the thorns and briars. And eventually he reaches the prize and wakes the beloved stranger, the most beautiful Princess in the world.

I associate with the Prince's weariness and torn hands, not to mention the sense of being caught in those brambles; struggling to escape we find there is no way back, we can only press on. But where are we heading, what or who is Beauty, if we take the place of the Prince? Is she the meaning of our quest, a purpose for our lives and our pains, or is Sleeping Beauty an image of God for us? But surely God does not slumber unawares? Of course, we can turn the story round and substitute God for the hero Prince. Then the Prince's search becomes a picture of God's longing to rescue us and the price he pays in the attempt. At one and the same time, I want to identify with the pilgrim Prince *and* the sleeping figure, waiting and waiting for the kiss.

The enduring strength of fairy stories is that they work at all sorts of levels. We can identify with several characters and explore all sorts of possibilities. Musing on a story which catches our imagination and seems to speak to us can offer revealing insights. So we can battle through the wild woods with God to reach the goal *and* know we are imprisoned and frozen, the one who needs to be touched by love and woken. Then Sleeping Beauty becomes an image of whatever represents the great prize for us; freedom, courage, hope, love, meaning, God; or the discovery of our true selves, our soul or inner life which has slumbered through the years. This is the gift of cancer for me, that through the fears and doubts has come the discovery that I am on a journey and that the journey has a goal. At a deeper level than I had imagined, I have found that this pilgrimage with God is what it means to me to be fully alive.

I have written in some detail about the retreat where I first began to understand the possibility of sharing in Christ's passion. Later that day, after the walk in the barley field, we were invited to attend a meditation in the chapel. The retreat was being held at a Roman Catholic convent and until now I had enjoyed this extra dimension of a different spirituality. Every evening there had been a period of silent prayer in front of the sacrament in a service called Benediction. Although this was new to me, I had found it a powerful and moving reminder of Christ's life given to and for us. On this, the Friday evening, we were invited to follow the Stations of the Cross, the final stages of Christ's journey to his death at Golgotha. Again this was unfamiliar to me, but I expected to be able to enter into the prayer, at least to some degree, as I had on previous nights. Later, I wrote: *There was a tape recording of readings and prayers playing, but it just seemed a lot of pious words to me. I felt as though we were indulging in a ghastly masochistic exercise, enjoying the agony and revelling in imaginary distress. The concentration on weakness and* *death seemed obscene. After a quarter of an hour or so, I left, feeling I had to get away from the stultifying conformity, and bolted out into the grounds. It was a grey, quiet, June dusk with a little high cloud and a glow from the sunset, low down in the West. There were planes streaking pink and silver over-head, we were quite close to Heathrow. I strode in fury to the furthest point of the huge grounds, and stood by a raggedy wire fence against the empty playing field – 'F*** you,' I yelled. 'I'm alive, I'm going to live. I will bloody well live to see my children's children. I WILL live!' I felt better, angry still, but better. The next day when I talked to my nun, she said: 'You passed through, through your passion to your own resurrection. Today you live. Today you are alive. Dying comes later, if it must, there will be time for all that. But today you are alive!'*

Yes, today I am alive, and it is a gift. There are others. The fragile, ever-fresh discovery that I am loved, not for what I do but simply for myself, remains a miracle. It is something that I find hard to comprehend and often forget, but that I am learn-ing is true. And too, I have found a tiny, growing, freedom to take control of my life, to choose to do or not do, rather than compulsively strive to fulfil others' expectations. Because I no longer have a job there is also the precious possibility of taking time to stop, to rest or to cherish the moment, to relax. I am aware what a great luxury this is, but I need to con-tinually remind myself and take permission to do so. The possibility is there, I have the choice.

It is not all pastoral idyll, of course and I get bored, frustrated and depressed like everybody else. But I am learn-ing, learning to *live*, rather than struggling to exist. The differ-ence is not that I am safe, or comfortable, or have the answers. I am not always sure how much I should take on, when to say 'No' and when to offer to help. I haven't got it all taped; I am not wonderfully mature or strong; my prayer life is variable and I make mistakes and hurt people's feelings, squabble and nag. The difference is that despite all my fears, anger and faithlessness, so far anyway, I am not alone. Not lost, after all,

* This surely is true of *all* people, of all faiths – not just Christians!

not wandering aimlessly or hounded by demons, but making a journey, walking the way with him, the one who is also wounded.

At present my cancer remains non-aggressive, but the prognosis is uncertain. It may remain sluggish or even disappear. It may become more aggressive in time and emerge in lungs, liver or brain resulting in premature death and statistically that is the likely outcome. Nobody seems prepared to say more than that. I have had long periods of comparative good health, particularly in the early days, but now my lack of energy has resulted in early retirement. This was a hard decision for me. I had moved on from working as university chaplain to full time work for the diocese, eventually as Head of the Vocations and Training Department. I had just taken up this post in 1996, when the cancer was discovered in my spine. After an operation and a few months off sick, I began the new job, but I struggled. I was eager to make a success of the post and there was much that I wanted to do, but I was continually frustrated by fatigue; days off were spent in bed and social life was constantly being cancelled. I began to feel that I was stupid to punish my body in this way, as well as being unfair to George and the rest of the family.

Within a year the cancer was discovered in other parts of my skeleton; not an immediate threat to life, as the damage it causes can be controlled by drugs, but *there*. I debated with myself and others: was I damaging my health by continuing work? Or would I be giving in, if I resigned? Or should I believe that God wanted me in the work and would supply the strength? In the early years I had insisted that cancer was not going to stop me doing anything and that, if there was a cost to my health, I was willing to take the risk. I wanted to go on living and working flat out and felt that this was part of my personality, the only way I *could* live. It has been painful to realize that I am physically unable to say that now and that my will is no longer enough to carry me forwards.

However, since I decided to retire, the relief has been immense. I have felt released from having to perform under pressure and it has been good to realize that I am no longer answerable, or carrying any great responsibility. I relish the space that retirement gives me and the opportunities but sometimes, unexpectedly, the regrets and disappointment catch me and I mind being on the sidelines. Although I know that a career is not the sum of my identity, I am having to learn a new way of being. Life feels good and infinitely precious; that does not mean that I do not have feelings of rebellion at the way my life is limited. But I am taken back over and over to the raw fact of our total dependence on God. It is still hard for me to ask for help, or admit my weakness. Although I look well, and enjoy my involvement in our home parish and else-where, I cannot work at full stretch and I have to keep goals fairly short-term. I find it hard to constantly repeat: 'I am well thank you, but I *do* get tired,' and feel frustrated when others respond by telling me that of course none of us are getting any younger! 'It is not like that. I mean *tired*, going-to-bed-for-the-day-tired,' I want to insist. But the smile and throw away remarks still come more easily. So I leave it.

Several years ago I had a dream which seemed immensely significant and which has stayed with me. In it I was walking along a path on a snowy afternoon, enjoying the sound and feel, but careful to watch my footing on the icy ground. The path turned and began to go downhill, gradually becoming steeper and more slippery until I turned off on to a tiny track. The snow was deeper here and heavier to wade through and I was still going down, though less steeply now. I began to be afraid. Walking was becoming hard work, the path was indistinct and uneven, with tussocks of grass under the snow and it was getting dark. I was relieved to arrive at a house, although when I went inside I found it bare and dingy. Inside was an oldish man in shabby, musty clothes. His face was kind, though yellow and lined, but the important thing about him was his eyes. They were clear and penetrating and the expression attracted and compelled me. Although I did not like the smell of decay around him, I was drawn by the sadness and love of his eyes. I knew that I had to stay there and assumed that I was supposed to marry him. The thought of kissing him was obscene, his teeth looked false and none too clean, but he assured me that he did not expect anything from me. Still, I felt obliged to show some warmth and steeled myself to kiss him. Then I awoke. At the time I was quite disturbed by this dream. Was I kinky? Was it about death or sex or both together? Should I have run screaming from the house? What happened next?

In my journal I noted: *I feel as if the dream was about recognizing the possibility of death. It's all very well being positive about living, but how will I deal with dying if/when I have to? I can't just ignore the fact of cancer, that seems to me to be stupid. There must surely be some gain, something to learn? I identify with the iciness in the dream. My feelings seem frozen as if I am unable to face what is happening. I can deal with life at the conscious, busy level quite well, and do; but I am aware of slips and slides and lurches going on somewhere deep down and a constant fear of coming crashing down, of being overwhelmed.*

I am angry with the easy way death is dismissed by Christians: 'We're all right! We have been given eternal life and expect the resurrection. We have nothing to fear!' They need to try it. George says that at the Hospice (where he had worked as chaplain) he saw no difference between Christians and non-Christians when it came to dying. Some patients were calm and peaceful, with or without faith; some were terrified, ditto. Though he also says that in all the time he worked there, not one person refused to allow him to pray for them. People were always glad of it and often visibly moved; not prayers for healing in the sense of cure, of course, but for peace, for God to be with them, for God's blessing on them. So perhaps they all died with faith, anyway. I do feel I want to understand, to take time to look, to use the fact that I have been warned of my mortality. I want to somehow make something of the actual experience of cancer and the invitation to journey. But when I stop to look at it, pain and depression envelop me.

* I agree. The prospect of life after death means nothing to me.

Some years on, I feel as though I understand the dream a little better, as well as feeling less crushed and terrified. As a whole, the dream spoke to me of being drawn towards the intuitive, the inner life, a more reflective and less active me. Certainly it was also about my sense of repulsion and protest that cancer had invaded my life, as well as my struggle to come to terms with an older and less perfect body. But the compulsion of those eyes, drawing and loving me, suggest that as I have been forced to embrace, rather than try to escape cancer, I may have found some treasure *in* it after all. When we face disaster we also begin a journey which, despite being sometimes unpleasant or uncomfortable, has a goal and a purpose. I do believe that God's intention is to give us a gift, to love us and bring us to life through the journeying; which is not to say that, given the choice, I would not have preferred to avoid the whole business!

I am reminded of my favourite of all the fairy tales, the other story with a Beauty in it, Beauty and the Beast. One interpretation suggests that Beauty can symbolize Christ, come to woo the human race and to make us beautiful and beloved. But I cannot see the story in that way. I have always identified with Beauty, trespassing in the garden, both repelled and fascinated by the Beast who imprisons her. And the Beast? Might he be the owner and creator, the lover-God himself? God hiding behind a rough disguise, hoping we will kiss him anyway; or kiss the place, the situation, that he has put us in and that confines us. If it *is* he who puts us there, of course? I seem to have come full circle! But if we will offer the kiss, then perhaps God can reveal himself as the perfect Prince; the one who knows and understands our reluctance to accept the scary externals of our situation and who patiently waits for us to realize that we are loved. And that all the trials and difficulties are strangely a part of the loving.

Of course we do not live in dreams or fairy tales, but they can offer encouragement and a perspective on our lives. They suggest that one day we might understand. 'Today you live. Today you are alive!' affirmed the kind nun on my retreat.

*I.e. learning to accept whatever fate brings you!

And I recognize that the call is to *live*; not waiting for things to get better, or worse; or making excuses for not living; or letting time drift past, but living. For me, that means living with my eyes open, conscious that I have an illness that as yet has no medical solution and bar miracles will end in my premature death. The challenge is to use the knowledge to live more fully and to go on using it in that way, whatever happens. I don't yet know if I am up to that. I do know that failure is allowed, or rather that what I think of as failure may not be so in God's eyes. All I have to do is what we all have to do, keep on keeping on, aware that I am currently not dying, but living.

Like all who try to live by faith, I want to believe that there is some meaning, some use that God makes of our pains; that he knows and is at work. I have to accept too that I could have got it wrong; that I may be deluded in thinking there is a purpose to discover, a direction and a God to travel the way with us. It may be so, there is no conclusive proof in either direction. But if God is a dream or an escape from reality, he is a very uncomfortable one; and if he does not exist then nothing much matters anyway and any illusion that can get me through the day will serve. But I choose to believe otherwise. Or rather, I do not have much choice about it, I cannot 'not believe'. So I may as well positively live as if it were all true and God *is*, and whether we know it or not, we are each on a journey towards God. Then we are being called into life, to become always more open to truth, more prepared to face ourselves. Then our difficulties and pains can be shared with God and may even be offered in the bearing of the cross with him. Although much is beyond our comprehension, we dare to offer all that we are; weakness, pain, failure, doubts and fears, as well as love and service, in the redemption of the world. And so we journey into life, in the hope that there will always be a still deeper love to be discovered.

Would you know our Lord's meaning in this? Learn it well. Love was his meaning . . . And so I saw full surely, that

before ever God made us, he loved us. And this love has
never faded nor ever shall. And in this love he has done all
his works, and in this love he has made all things profitable
for us, and in this love our life is everlasting . . . All this we
shall see in God, without end. Which Jesus grant us. Amen.[9]

(a)

It is not a question of
believing in God or
something else —
it is believing in God
or nothing else!

Appendix: Practical Matters

The following brief points may be just the thing to send you into a paroxysm of rage and the book hurtling across the room, in which case I am delighted to be providing a useful focus for your frustration. But I hope that some may reach the spot, or give you some ideas about how best to deal with your feelings and situation; not to mention coping with other people.

Support

- Accept practical offers of help: lifts, ironing, cooked dishes, treats. People *want* to do something and feel helpless and guilty because they are not going through all that you are. It is a kindness to allow them to give to you. If you can bear to receive, it feels good.
- Use the organizations provided for your particular situation. The Citizens' Advice Bureau or local library should be able to suggest those with specialized expertise. Many agencies provide telephone Help Lines which are invaluable for niggling questions. They will gladly provide leaflets and sources of more information.
- Let your GP know if you feel unable to cope, or get very depressed. Short-term anti-depressants may help you through. They do not mean you are a weakling or failure. Also your GP's surgery may be able to offer counselling, or further help.
- Find a 'buddy', someone you can complain to endlessly and who will not judge you. This may be your partner or

another family member or good friend. But sometimes those who love us best are too swamped with their own reactions to be able to give us what we need. If no one comes to mind, use the professional help available – local GP, counselling service, or clergy should be able to offer support or pointers to those who can.

- Practise being assertive. That simply means saying how it is; what you want and don't want and what is making you angry or distressed. If you are worried about a forthcoming interview with lawyer, ex-partner, doctor or colleague – practise with a friend. Go through what you plan to say and let them comment. This will help you avoid coming across as either aggressive or timid and apologetic. The idea is to communicate clearly so that you are heard and understood.

- You might find some sort of Healing Service helpful. Your local church should be able to let you know details of any in the area. But do take someone with you, in case it is not your scene – and do shop around. Some people feel most comfortable with formal worship, some with informal, some in the anonymity of a large gathering and some only in small intimate situations. What matters is what works for you. Regular prayer can be a great source of strength, so don't feel that you should not be prayed for repeatedly for the same problem, or condition etc. That is not about lack of faith, but the contrary.

- Relaxation techniques are helpful in maximizing your energy and feelings of wellbeing. There is also evidence that for some conditions they can facilitate cure/healing. All sorts of disciplines are available, Christian, secular, or those based on other spiritualities. Your local church may be able to help with basic teaching, or supply details of places/individuals who could offer these. A Medical Centre or library may also offer a variety of opportunities. But do be aware that, if you are ill or in a low state, you are vulnerable. Be sure not to be exploited financially or in other ways.

- Alternative medicines and therapies and suggestions about diet and/or dietary supplements are now very well-documented. Many Christians use them and benefit, some are less at ease with some forms of alternative therapy. Again, be aware that you are vulnerable – seek advice and pick and choose.

- Accept that is it OK to refuse to talk about things if/when you don't want to. Try changing the subject. If people persist, tell them that you need the chance to think about something else. Most people are unsure whether to mention a sensitive subject and want guidance from you. Similarly, if you *do* need to talk, ask if they are happy to listen for a bit. Most will feel honoured to be of use.
- Consider joining a Support Group. These come in all types from 'Compassionate Friends' to 'Cancer Support'. If you don't like it, leave it.

The professionals

- Take someone with you to the doctor/lawyer. Writing questions down before you go in and giving a copy to your companion can be useful. You can then brief them to nudge you with: 'Didn't you also want to ask . . . ?', in case you lose your nerve. It is also helpful to write down the answers you receive. It is extremely difficult to take in detailed or unfamiliar information when you are dealing with turbulent emotions and you can easily forget details. If you feel embarrassed, say: 'I have been advised to jot down some notes . . .'
- Insist that language is used that you understand and ask for clarification if you are unsure. Don't be embarrassed. There are areas of knowledge where you are the expert and the professional in front of you would be totally lost – even if only the intricacies of your family history! This person is there for you, so make them work *for* you.
- If you are less than 100% happy with your medical care – ask for a second opinion. Your GP can organize this for you at a hospital/centre of your choice. Your original consultant will not be informed, so if you choose to go back to her/him

you need not be embarrassed. You will then have the benefit of an independent opinion about your treatment so far. You may change consultants if you wish. Don't take 'crap' from anyone.

- There are well-documented differences in the standard of care and expertise that you can expect for certain medical conditions in particular centres. Breast cancer is among them. Initially you will no doubt go to your local hospital, probably too distressed and shocked to think more about it. But specialist centres have better results, offer the most go-ahead treatment options and staff who are specialists. Use them. Regulations about where you can seek treatment change, but if you are prepared to enquire and insist you should be able to get what you want. Your GP will want to help and your local MP can be a useful source of influence. That is what they are there for.

Be nice to yourself

- Don't expect too much of yourself in terms of energy or stamina, when you have had an emotional shock. Exhaustion is a common and normal response and may last for some time.
- Look for little things to cheer you up, small comforts to get you through the hour or day. Accept them as signs that you are loved and held. God *is* there.
- Don't expect to be able to pray, unless you *want* to. Let others pray on your behalf. Your job is to be carried, loved and cradled. You probably will not feel any of those things but you don't have to add guilt about a low spiritual state to your other difficulties. It is normal.
- Keeping a journal of your feelings and thoughts can be a great help. This is private, for you to record whatever you feel – rage, hatred, self-pity, envy – better out than in. It also helps you to clarify what you want at any particular time; whether it is to tell someone how you feel or to run away and forget it all for the day. Take action if possible.

- You do not have to listen to other people's theories about why you are ill, or why some terrible thing has befallen you. You certainly should not listen when others' views hurt or offend you, albeit unknowingly. If you feel unable to confront them, ask a friend to have a quiet word. Protect yourself from unnecessary stress; you do not need it.

- Talk to your family/close friends. You may need to explain that you do not want them to solve the problem, only to allow you to say how you feel. Even if this is difficult for them, and you need other regular support, you need to have told them how it is for you. You may also need to say the important things – that you love them, that you have forgiven this or that. Do it, write the letter, make the call. You will feel better for it.

- Feel free to protect yourself from people and situations that are too difficult. Some people are always hard to handle, you don't need them now. Be asleep or out, leave the phone off the hook, or ask someone to take the calls for you. You don't even have to answer the door. If that feels dreadful, leave a note on it saying you are resting. People will understand and might even be relieved. They are busy too.

- Try going on a retreat, take a friend with you if you like. There are all kinds available – Christian, secular or other faiths. Some are structured, some not, and can last for anything from a weekend to thirty days (not recommended for the beginner!). They are generally set within a pattern of prayer and offer peace and quiet for reflection in fairly basic accommodation, often at stunningly beautiful venues. 'Individually Guided Retreats' with a time to meet regularly each day with a retreat guide, but no other input, are generally for a minimum of four days and often take the traditional eight days. Other sorts of silent retreat have a director who gives some talks each day and will see you for a discussion if you like. Many retreats now offer opportunities for creativity – painting/clay/writing/embroidery/ calligraphy etc. Some retreats have particular themes and may offer walks/visits to local beauty spots etc. And these are only the Christian variety. A Christian bookshop should have publications listing Retreat Houses and their calendar of events.

- If/when you have the energy, take up something creative, or some activity you have always wanted to do. Experiment, take a risk, join a new group, have a go.

- You do not have to read/watch/listen to everything that is offered. I remember a friend catching me in tears while reading a helpful book that suggested that at some level I *needed* cancer. Her comment: 'Throw the damn book way' remains a healthy option – including this one, of course.

- I advise you to use the following phrase freely: 'I have been advised'. Whether it is not to push yourself/to take time off/to go to a Support Group/to remain closeted with your closest family – whatever. People will assume that you have been advised by an expert and this may give you permission to do what you need to do.

- Because you have had a particular experience, this does not mean that you have to take on everyone else in a similar situation. Be honest with yourself about what you can cope with. There is no point in getting bogged down in situations that are too painful or that drain you; you will only become exhausted and depressed. That does not make you a failure, but someone mature enough to recognizes her/his limitations.

- Do something good for your body. Spoil it by taking up gentle and enjoyable exercise, or having a massage or facial, or some really good meals – pay extra for tempting and healthy options. This *is* the rainy day. Sex is good for you too, if you feel well enough.

- Rest. Do nothing. Listen to your body and allow it to dictate what you do and do not do. If you can afford it, take some sort of a holiday, preferably one that allows relaxation, rather than viewing the pyramids!

- Have regular treats. These need not be extravagant – an outing, a day away, an afternoon watching an old movie, or seeing friends that you really enjoy.

- Remember: YOU ARE NOT RESPONSIBLE FOR OTHER PEOPLE'S REACTIONS TO YOUR DOING WHATEVER IS NECESSARY FOR YOU, TODAY.

Notes

1. *Cancer – The Shock*

1. C. S. Lewis, *A Grief Observed*, Faber 1961, p. 7.
2. Ibid., p. 9.
3. Ibid., p. 38.
4. Mary Craig, *Blessings*, Hodder 1979, pp. 141–42.
5. Matt. 5.3, 4, 10.
6. Abbé de Tourville, *Letters of Direction*, Dacre Press/A. and C. Black 1939, p. 69.

2. *Whose Fault Is It Anyway?*

1. Rom. 8.28.
2. Luke 18.9–14.
3. Harold S. Kushner, *When Bad Things Happen to Good People*, Pan Books 1981, p. 50.
4. Rom. 12.15.
5. Isa. 45.7.
6. Hos. 6.1.
7. John 9.3.
8. Matt. 12.22–26; Mark 9.17–29; Luke 10.17–19.
9. Matt. 13.28.
10. II Cor. 12.7.
11. II Cor. 4.10; Phil. 3.10.
12. I Peter 4.12,13
13. Jer. 31.3.
14. Isa. 43.4.
15. Hos. 2.14,15.
16. Ps. 84.6.
17. Ex. 16.15.
18. From *Revelations of Divine Love*, ch.68. Taken from *Enfolded in Love. Daily Readings with Julian of Norwich* ed Robert Llewelyn, Darton, Longman and Todd 1980, 1999, p. 39. Translation by Martin Glasscoe.
19. Helen Waddell, *Peter Abelard*, Collins Fount 1977, pp. 240–42.

3. *The Cross at the Centre of the Universe*

1. Job 38.4, 22, 26, 28; 39.26.
2. Karen Armstrong, *A History of God*, Ballantine Books, New York 1993, p. 376.
3. Jer. 8.21.
4. Isa. 63.9.
5. John 1.29.
6. Luke 23.34.
7. Jürgen Moltmann, *The Crucified God*, SCM Press 1974, p. 278.
8. Hans Küng, *On Being a Christian*, Collins 1977; SCM Press 1995, p. 396.
9. II Cor. 5.19.
10. Col. 1.17–20: I Peter 1.20.
11. Dorothy L. Sayers, *The Man Born to be King. A Play-Cycle on the Life of our Lord and Saviour, Jesus Christ*, Gollancz 1946, p. 340.
12. Helen Waddell, *Peter Abelard*, Collins Fount 1977, pp. 252–53.

4. *Does God Heal?*

1. Mark 2.5; Luke 17. 11–19.
2. Mark 1.33; John 5.3–7; Matt. 13.58.
3. Mark 7.24ff.; John 11.4–6.
4. Mark 6.1–6.
5. Mark 2.1–12, 5.12–15, 10.46ff.; Luke 7.11–17, 8.40–48; John 4.46ff.
6. Matt. 6.33.
7. Luke 8. 49–56.
8. Rom 8.28.
9. Reginald East, *Heal the Sick*, Hodder 1977, p. 117.
10. I Cor. 15.19.
11. John 21.28.
12. Rev. 21.3,4.
13. Col. 1.24.
14. Matt. 10.30

5. *Wholeness*

1. John Galsworthy, *The Forsyte Saga*, conclusion to Book 3, *To Let*, Heinemann 1921 and many subsequent editions.
2. C. S. Lewis, *Till We Have Faces. A Myth Retold*, Collins Fount 1978, pp. 302–5.
3. C. S. Lewis, *The Last Battle*, Puffin Books 1974, p. 20.
4. Ezek. 3.15. Margin.
5. From *Revelations of Divine Love*, chs 39, 82, 68. Taken from *Enfolded in Love. Daily Readings with Julian of Norwich*, Darton, Longman and Todd 1980, pp. 17, 54, 40.
6. I John 3.2.

7. C. S. Lewis, *Till We Have Faces*, p. 291.
8. Ibid., pp. 307–8.

6. *Is There Any Meaning in All of This?*

1. Gerard Manley Hopkins (1844–89), 'As kingfishers catch fire'.
2. Victor E. Frankl, *Man's Search for Meaning*, Washington Square Press 1984, pp. 95–97.
3. Ibid., p. 136.
4. Elie Wiesel, *All Rivers Run to the Sea. Memoirs*, HarperCollins 1996, pp. 79–80.
5. Victor E. Frankl, *Man's Search for Meaning*, pp. 170, 99.
6. Jürgen Moltmann, *The Crucified God*, SCM Press 1974, p. 278.
7. Harold S. Kushner, *When Bad Things Happen to Good People*, Pan Books 1981, p. 154.
8. Gen. 32.26.
9. Hans Küng, *On Being a Christian*, Collins 1977; SCM Press 1995, p. 433.
10. Deut. 30.19.
11. From *Revelations of Divine Love*, ch.86. Taken from *Enfolded in Love. Daily Readings with Julian of Norwich*, Darton, Longman and Todd 1980, p. 59.

7. *Carrying the Cross*

1. Luke 23.26.
2. Phil. 3.7–10.
3. II Cor. 6.4,5.
4. II Cor.12.7.
5. Col. 1.14.
6. Luke 18.1; I Cor.1.26; I Peter 4.13,14.
7. Acts 9.4, 22.7, 26.14.
8. Victor E. Frankl. *Man's Search for Meaning*, Washington Square Press 1984, p. 136.
9. Elie Wiesel. *All Rivers Run to the Sea. Memoirs*, HarperCollins 1996, p. 183.
10. Frankl, op.cit., pp. 161–62.
11. Ibid., p. 175.
12. Mary Craig, *Blessings*, Hodder 1979, p. 144.
13. Mark 8.34; John 1.25, 26; II Cor. 4.11, 12.10; Gal. 2.19,20; Phil. 3.10,11; Col. 1.24.
14. Mark 10.39.
15. John 21.18.
16. Jürgen Moltmann, *The Crucified God*, SCM Press 1974, pp. 45–46.
17. Sister Eileen Lyddon, *Door through Darkness. St John of the Cross and Mysticism in Everyday Life*, New City 1994, pp. 158,162.

8. Acceptance

1. *Bernard of Clairvaux*, Devotional Classics Series ed Richard J. Foster and James Bryan Smith, Hodder 1993, p. 55.
2. Matt. 18.2.
3. T. H. White, *The Once and Future King*, Collins 1958; Collins Fontana 1962, pp. 190–92.
4. Ibid., p. 191.
5. II Cor. 12.10.
6. Phil. 4.13.
7. Mark 1.38.
8. John 4.6.
9. John 12.7.
10. Matt. 26.12; Mark 14.8.
11. W. H. Vanstone, *The Stature of Waiting*, Darton, Longman and Todd 1982, p. 20.
12. Ibid., p. 28.
13. Gal. 5.22.
14. Sheila Cassidy, *Audacity to Believe*, Collins 1977, pp. 230–31.
15. Sister Eileen Lyddon (quoting from St John of the Cross), *Door through Darkness. St John of the Cross and Mysticism in Everyday Life*, New City 1994, p. 159.
16. John 19.26–30.
17. Luke 23.34, 43, 46.
18. Matt. 27.46, 50; Mark 15.34, 37.
19. John 19.41.
20. Matt. 25.40.
21. I John 3.2.

9. Today I Am Alive

1. Deut. 8.11, 15, 16.
2. William Nicholson, *Shadowlands*, Revised Version, Samuel French 1992, p. 2.
3. Jer. 18.6.
4. C. S. Lewis, *A Grief Observed*, Faber 1961, p. 26.
5. John 14.20.
6. Heb. 11.8.
7. From *Revelations of Divine Love*, ch.82. Taken from *Enfolded in Love. Daily Readings with Julian of Norwich*, Darton, Longman and Todd 1980.
8. Arthur Hugh Clough (1819–61), 'Say not, the struggle nought availeth' in, e.g., *The Oxford Book of English Verse*, OUP 1972, p. 681.
9. Julian of Norwich, *Revelations of Divine Love*, ch. 86. Taken from *Enfolded in Love*, pp. 59–60.

Acknowledgments

The author and publishers are grateful to the following for permission to use copyright material:

Constable Publishers Ltd for extracts from *Peter Abelard* by Helen Waddell, published 1933 by Constable.

Continuum Publishing Group for an extract from *The Man Born to be King* by Dorothy L. Sayers, published 1946 by Victor Gollancz.

Darton, Longman and Todd Ltd for extracts from *Enfolded in Love* edited by Robert Llewelyn, published and copyright 1980 and 1999 by Darton, Longman and Todd; and *The Stature of Waiting* by W. H. Vanstone, published and copyright 1982 by Darton, Longman and Todd.

The Estate of C. S. Lewis for extracts from *Till We Have Faces*, published 1978 by Collins Fount.

HarperCollins Publishers Ltd for extracts from Elie Wiesel, *All Rivers Run to the Sea* and Sheila Cassidy, *Audacity to Believe*.

David Higham Associates for an extract from *The Once and Future King* by T. H. White, published 1958 by HarperCollins.

Hodder and Stoughton Ltd for extracts from *Blessings* by Mary Craig.

SCM Press for extracts from *On Being a Christian* by Hans Küng and *The Crucified God* by Jürgen Moltmann.

Simon & Schuster, Inc, New York, for extracts from *Man's Search for Meaning* by Victor E. Frankl, published 1984 by Washington Square Press.